Student Edition

Social Studies Alive!®
Our Community and Beyond

TCi™

Chief Executive Officer
Bert Bower

Chief Operating Officer
Amy Larson

Director of Product Development
Maria Favata

Strategic Product Manager
Nathan Wellborne

Content Developer
Ginger Wu

Senior Strategic Editor
Kim Merlino

Program Editors and Writers
Mikaila Garfinkel
Alex White
Ginger Wu

Production Manager
Jodi Forrest

Operations & Software Manager
Marsha Ifurung

Designer
Sarah Osentowski

Art Direction
Julia Foug

Teachers' Curriculum Institute
PO Box 1327
Rancho Cordova, CA 95741

Customer Service: 800-497-6138
www.teachtci.com

ISBN 978-1-58371-136-1
1 2 3 4 5 6 7 8 9 10 -WC- 20 19 18 17 16 15

Manufactured by Webcrafters, Inc., Madison, WI
United States of America, March 2015, Job# 120963

SUSTAINABLE
FORESTRY
INITIATIVE

Certified Sourcing
www.sfiprogram.org
SFI-00617

Program Consultant

Vicki LaBoskey, Ph.D.
Professor of Education
Mills College, Oakland, California

Reading Specialist

Barbara Schubert, Ph.D.
Reading Specialist
Saint Mary's College, Moraga, California

Social Studies Content Scholars

Paul A. Barresi, J.D., Ph.D.
Professor of Political Science and
Environmental Law
*Southern New Hampshire University,
Manchester, New Hampshire*

Phillip J. VanFossen, Ph.D.
James F. Ackerman Professor of Social
Studies Education and Associate Director,
Purdue Center for Economic Education
Purdue University, West Lafayette, Indiana

Fred Walk
Lecturer, Department of Geography
Instructional Assistant Professor,
Department of History
Illinois State University, Normal, Illinois

Wyatt Wells, Ph.D.
Professor of History
Auburn Montgomery, Alabama

Literature Consultant

Regina M. Rees, Ph.D.
Assistant Professor
*Beeghly College of Education, Youngstown
State University, Youngstown, Ohio*

Teacher Consultants

Judy Brodigan
Elementary Social Studies Supervisor
Lewisville Independent School District, Texas

Lynn Casey
Teacher
*Husmann Elementary School, Crystal Lake,
Illinois*

Ann Dawson
Educational Consultant and Intermediate
Curriculum Specialist
Gahanna, Ohio

Debra Elsen
Teacher
Manchester Elementary, Manchester, Maryland

Candetta Holdren
Teacher
Linlee Elementary, Lexington, Kentucky

Shirley Jacobs
Library Media Specialist
*Irving Elementary School, Bloomington,
Illinois*

Elizabeth McKenna
Teacher
*St. Thomas Aquinas Catholic School, Diocese
of Orlando, Florida*

Mitch Pascal
Social Studies Specialist
Arlington County Schools, Arlington, Virginia

Becky Suthers
Retired Teacher
*Stephen F. Austin Elementary, Weatherford,
Texas*

Lisa West
Instructional Specialist,
Language Arts/Social Studies
Landis Elementary School, Houston, Texas

Tiffany Wilson
Teacher
Corbell Elementary, Frisco, Texas

Beth Yankee
Teacher
*The Woodward School for Technology and
Research, Kalamazoo, Michigan*

English Language Arts & Literacy and *Social Studies Alive!*

Social Studies Alive! is aligned with the Common Core State Standards for English Language Arts & Literacy[1] (CCELA) to ensure that students develop literacy skills through learning social studies. The K–5 CCELA are organized around four college and career readiness strands: reading, writing, speaking and listening, and language.

Key Points from the ELA Common Core	*Social Studies Alive!*
Reading	
Informational and literary texts should be balanced, with at least 50 percent of reading time devoted to expository texts.	*Social Studies Alive!* reflects this balance in the Student Text. Each lesson has several sections of purely informational text that explain the content of that lesson, followed by a Reading Further article that blends literary and informational style text to engage students.
There is a "staircase" of increasing complexity in what students must be able to read as they move throughout the grades.	*Social Studies Alive!* is written with close attention paid to the text complexity, with increasingly sophisticated text as students progress through the grades. However, within each grade's text, there is variation in the complexity to ensure that there is challenging text for all students.
Close reading of text is used to identify main ideas, supporting details, and evidence.	*Social Studies Alive!* Reading Notes in the Interactive Student Notebook require students to answer questions using evidence from the text and require a clear understanding of the main ideas and other details provided in the section.
Writing	
Routine production of writing appropriate for a range of tasks, purposes, and audiences is emphasized.	From the earliest grades, *Social Studies Alive!* students practice three types of writing—writing to persuade, writing to inform or explain, and writing to convey experience. For example, when they record Reading Notes, students enjoy the challenges of writing about a personal experience related to the lesson, creating timelines, and writing song lyrics.
Effective use of evidence is central throughout the writing standards.	*Social Studies Alive!* students are expected to use evidence appropriately to support their analysis, reflections, and research. They are given support in identifying key details, which will serve most effectively as evidence. They also reflect on the role evidence plays in the social sciences and argument in general.

[1]National Governors Association Center for Best Practices, Council of Chief State School Officers. *Common Core State Standards for English Language Arts & Literacy in History/Social Studies, Science, and Technical Subjects.* National Governors Association Center for Best Practices, Council of Chief State School Officers, Washington D.C. Date: 2010.

Key Points from the ELA Common Core	Social Studies Alive!
Speaking and Listening	
Participation in rich, structured academic conversations in one-on-one, small-group, and whole class situations is emphasized.	The teaching strategies in *Social Studies Alive!* provide varied grouping techniques, resulting in a balance of paired, small group, and whole class discussions in which students reflect on their experiences and understanding of the activities. These discussions are designed to build clear communication skills that are critical to success in social studies and for college and career readiness.
Contributing accurate, relevant information; responding to and building on what others have said; and making comparisons and contrasts are important skills for productive conversations.	The cooperative tolerant classroom conventions emphasized throughout all of TCI's curricula encourage students to respond to and build on ideas and arguments presented by other students. During discussions, *Social Studies Alive!* guides students to compare and contrast relevant experiences across the four disciplines of social studies.
Language	
Students should acquire and use general academic and domain-specific words.	*Social Studies Alive!* has a progression of increasingly sophisticated vocabulary built into it. Key terms are used throughout a lesson or the year without overwhelming students with too many unfamiliar words. Every component of *Social Studies Alive!* makes use of the vocabulary and includes activities to help solidify comprehension.
Skills to determine or clarify the meaning of unknown words or phrases are essential.	*Social Studies Alive!* vocabulary terms are previewed at the beginning of the lesson and students complete vocabulary development assignments, such as a Word Parts Log, that trains students to parse words to infer meaning.
Students should demonstrate command of standard English, including grammar, punctuation, and spelling.	Throughout all components of *Social Studies Alive!*, students are expected to demonstrate command of the conventions of written and spoken English. An Editing and Proofreading Checklist is included to help students write with minimal errors.

Considerate Text

Social Studies Alive! is both engaging and helps students read text that is more complex and at a higher level. That's because our authors wrote it as a "considerate text," which is another way of saying that it makes readers want to read it. Here are some ways this book is considerate for all levels of readers.

Short sections, each with an informative title, make it easier for readers to understand and remember the most important points.

Captions for photos, illustrations, and maps reinforce the main idea of the section and provide details about the picture.

Thoughtfully selected large images illustrate the main idea and support visual learners.

1. Countries Trade What They Have for What They Want

Have you ever traded things with your friends? Maybe you traded an apple for a banana at lunch. Or maybe you traded a toy for a game. Why did you trade with your friend?

When people trade with one another, they trade things they have for things that they want. Different countries can trade with each other, too. For example, Ecuador is a country that trades with the United States. Ecuador grows lots of bananas. The United States does not grow bananas, but people in the United States want to eat them. So the United States buys bananas from Ecuador.

What does Ecuador want? Farmers in Ecuador need tractors. The United States has many factories that make tractors. So Ecuador buys tractors from the United States.

Bananas from Ecuador can be traded for tractors from the United States.

The section is written with a clear focus on the main idea. Information is presented in easy-to-manage chunks for better understanding.

Ecuador sells bananas to the United States. The United States sells tractors to Ecuador. You could say that Ecuador trades its bananas for tractors. In the same way, the United States trades its tractors for bananas.

These kinds of trades go on all over the world. Countries have traded with one another for hundreds of years. This is called **global trade**. Today, global trade is bigger than ever before. One reason for this is that people have figured out better ways to move and store goods.

As global trade grows, countries around the world rely on each other more and more. The United States wants bananas, and Ecuador has more bananas than it wants. Ecuador wants more tractors, and the United States has more tractors than it wants. The United States and Ecuador can now trade with one another, and both countries are better off.

Many goods travel on container ships like this one.

global trade the buying and selling of goods and services between countries around the world

Important new social studies words are in bold type. These words are defined in the margin and in the glossary.

Single-column text makes it easier to read. Paragraphs end at the bottom of the page instead of continuing on the next page.

The United States and Global Trade **189**

The Four Core Disciplines of Social Studies

Each of the four core disciplines identified by the National Council for the Social Studies in its C3 Framework[2] has a unique set of ideas, tools, and ways of thinking. Each lesson of *Social Studies Alive!* is aligned to one or more of these disciplines.

 Civics

Important ideas of civics are based on understanding government at various levels, the political system, rules and laws, civic engagement, and democratic principles.

 Economics

The idea of "resources" as including human, physical, and natural resources is essential for understanding the economic decisions people, businesses, and governments make in local, national, and global markets.

[2]National Council for the Social Studies (NCSS), *The College, Career, and Civic Life (C3) Framework for Social Studies State Standards: Guidance for Enhancing the Rigor of K–12 Civics, Economics, Geography, and History* (Silver Spring, MD: NCSS, 2013).

Geography

Using maps and other representations of Earth, understanding the relationship between culture and the environment, analyzing how human populations change, and learning that some environmental changes occur on a global scale are all essential aspects of geography.

History

Reasoning about chronological patterns, explaining how people's perspectives can change, working with historical sources, identifying causes and effects, and developing claims from evidence are some of the skills students develop as they study history.

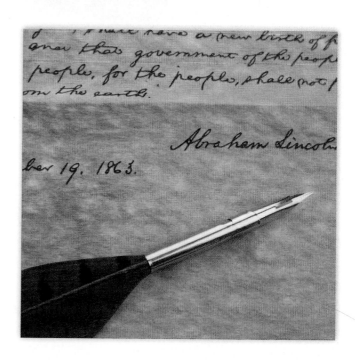

Look for the discipline icons at the beginning of each lesson and Reading Further.

How to Use this Program

Welcome to *Social Studies Alive! Our Community and Beyond,* where students learn about citizenship and how the geography and economics of their local community relates to the world around it.

1 The teacher begins each lesson with a **Presentation** that previews the lesson and facilitates one or more minds-on or hands-on activities.

2 In the Presentations, students participate in an interactive **activity** that connects to English Language Arts literacy by using the tools of social studies inquiry: asking questions, using sources and other evidence to develop claims, and communicating conclusions.

3a In the online **Student Subscription,** students expand their knowledge through reading the Student Text and processing what they have learned in the **Interactive Student Notebook.** Students can also play a game-like **Reading Challenge** activity.

3b Alternatively, students can read from the **Student Edition** and complete a consumable Interactive Student Notebook.

4 The lesson ends with students demonstrating their knowledge of the core ideas and essential social studies skills of the lesson through a variety of paper and online **assessments.**

How to Read the Table of Contents

The table of contents is your guide to *Social Studies Alive! Our Community and Beyond*. It lists all the lessons in your text and other resources, such as an in-depth look at what it means to be a citizen.

The **lesson title** tells you the overall topic of the lesson.

Every lesson emphasizes one or more of the four **core disciplines** of social studies: Civics, Economics, Geography, and History.

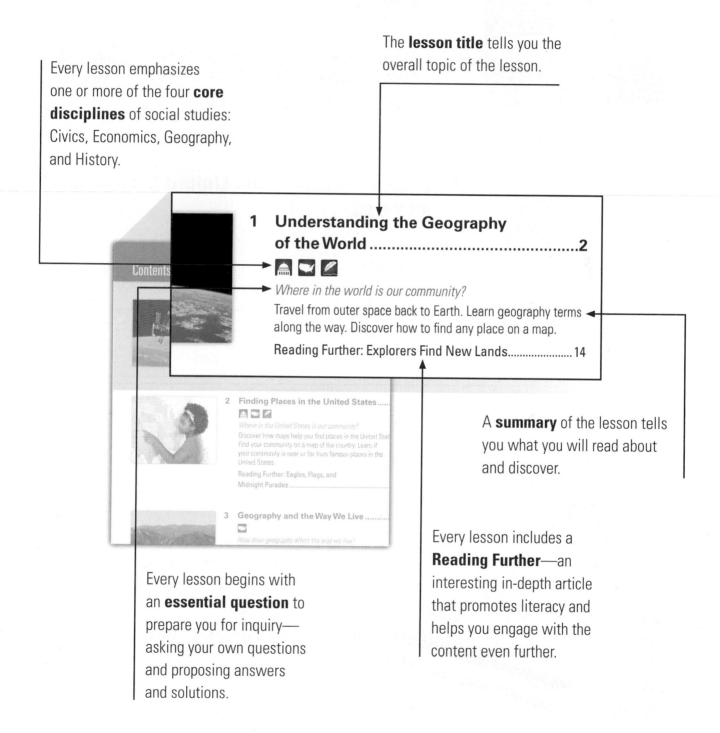

1 Understanding the Geography of the World................................**2**

Where in the world is our community?
Travel from outer space back to Earth. Learn geography terms along the way. Discover how to find any place on a map.

Reading Further: Explorers Find New Lands.....................14

2 Finding Places in the United States.....
Where in the United States is our community?
Discover how maps help you find places in the United States. Find your community on a map of the country. Learn if your community is near or far from famous places in the United States.
Reading Further: Eagles, Flags, and Midnight Parades..........

3 Geography and the Way We Live..........
How does geography affect the way we live?

A **summary** of the lesson tells you what you will read about and discover.

Every lesson includes a **Reading Further**—an interesting in-depth article that promotes literacy and helps you engage with the content even further.

Every lesson begins with an **essential question** to prepare you for inquiry— asking your own questions and proposing answers and solutions.

Contents

Citizenship Throughout the Day 296

Read about the meaning of citizenship. Find out what it means to be a good citizen at school, in your community, and at home.

The State of Florida

Maps

Primary Sources

A primary source of an event is an object created by someone who was there. See for yourself what you can learn about history from old photos, notebooks, certificates, and other primary sources.

Understanding the Geography of the World

Where in the world is our community?

Introduction

Picture yourself as an astronaut in a space shuttle. If you looked at the planet Earth from space, what do you think you would see? Maybe clouds, land, and water? What would you need to know to find your landing site on Earth?

To answer these questions, you need to know some geography. Geography is the study of Earth—its land, water, air, and people. In this lesson, you will learn about how Earth can be divided into different pieces.

You will come across important geography vocabulary words, such as *hemispheres, continents, countries,* and *states.* These words describe pieces that make up Earth. They will also help you use maps to find any place on Earth—from space or from your classroom.

Social Studies Vocabulary
border
capital
city
continent
country
equator
geography
government
ocean
prime meridian

◀ From space you can see much of the Earth. Where on Earth do you live?

Civics Geography

You can only see half of Earth at a time. Half of a sphere is known as a hemisphere.

geography the study of Earth—its spaces, land, water, air, and people

1. Our Community Is on Planet Earth

Remember that you are an astronaut in outer space. From your space shuttle, you can see how big Earth looks outside your window. You will see clouds, water, and land. You may also see mountains, deserts, and other things on Earth. These are all part of Earth's **geography**.

How would you describe the shape of Earth? Earth is not flat. Instead, you may notice that Earth is shaped like a ball. What else is shaped like a ball? Another word for an object shaped like a ball is sphere. If you cut a sphere in half, you get two hemispheres. Hemisphere means half of a sphere. Earth is broken up into several hemispheres.

Imagine a line around the middle of Earth, like a belt that goes around your waist. Many maps of Earth have a line like this called the **equator**. The equator divides Earth into the Northern Hemisphere and the Southern Hemisphere.

You can also divide a sphere from top to bottom. Imagine a line that starts at the top of Earth at the North Pole and runs down one side of Earth to the bottom at the South Pole. There is a special line like this on maps of Earth. It passes through the city of Greenwich, in England. We call this line the **prime meridian**. It divides Earth into the Western Hemisphere and the Eastern Hemisphere.

Find the equator and the prime meridian on the maps. How many hemispheres do you see?

equator the imaginary line that divides Earth into the Northern and Southern hemispheres

prime meridian the imaginary line that divides Earth into the Eastern and Western hemispheres

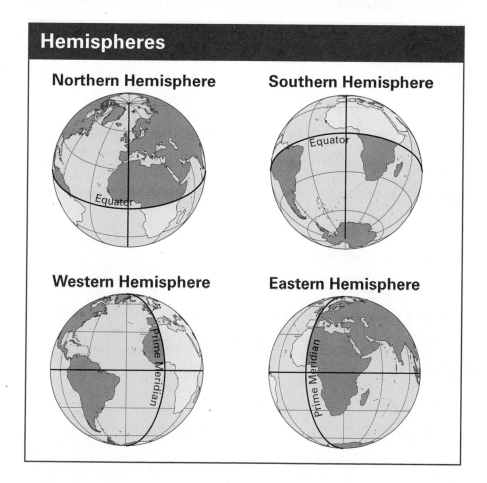

Hemispheres

Northern Hemisphere

Southern Hemisphere

Western Hemisphere

Eastern Hemisphere

The equator separates the Northern and Southern Hemispheres, while the prime meridian divides the Western and Eastern hemispheres. Which hemispheres are you a part of?

ocean one of the five largest bodies of water on Earth

continent one of the seven large bodies of land on Earth

Earth consists of land and sea. The land is divided into continents, and the sea is divided into oceans.

2. Our Community Is on a Continent

From space, you can see that most of Earth is covered with water. The largest bodies of water are called **oceans**.

There are five oceans on Earth. They are called the Pacific Ocean, the Atlantic Ocean, the Indian Ocean, the Southern Ocean, and the Arctic Ocean. Look at the map to find the five oceans.

The oceans wrap around large bodies of land. These areas of land are called **continents**.

There are seven continents on Earth. They are called Africa, Antarctica, Asia, Australia, Europe, North America, and South America.

Oceans and Continents

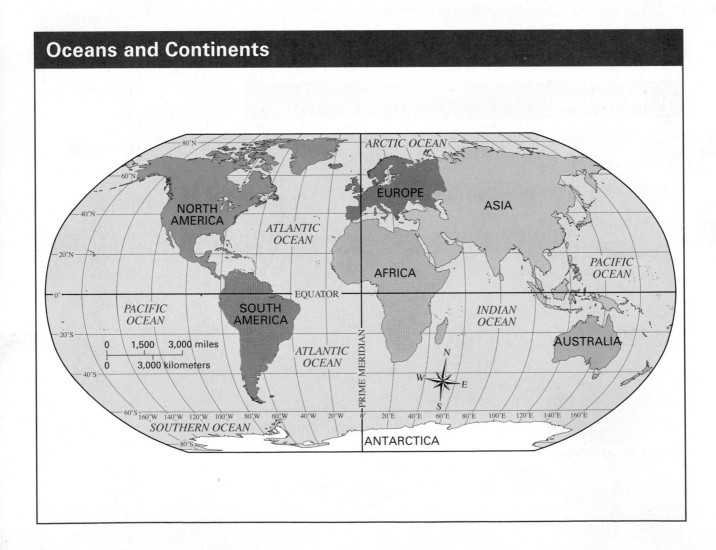

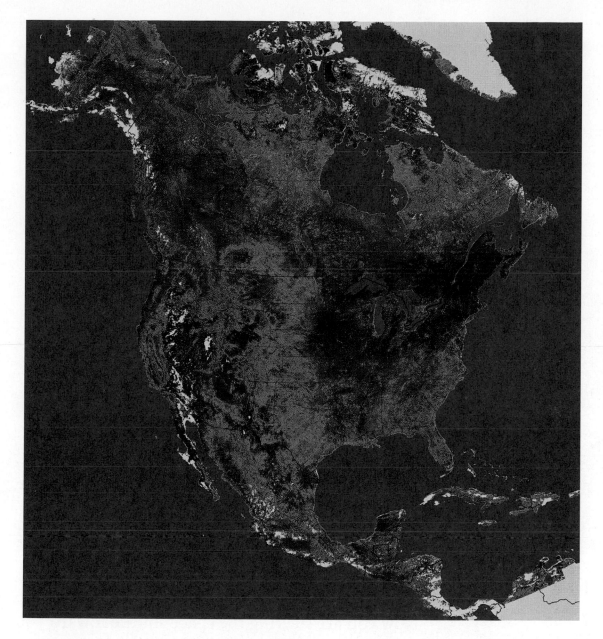

Asia is the largest continent, and Australia is the smallest. You can look at a map to find each of the seven continents. You can see that each continent has a different color on the map.

Each continent also has its own shape. The continents are mostly surrounded by oceans, but many of them are connected to each other by land in certain places.

On which continent do you live? Do you live near an ocean?

Each of the seven continents looks different. Which continent is this?

Where on this continent is the country that you are going to land your space shuttle?

country an area of land that has its own government

government a group that helps run a community, state, or country

3. Our Community Is in a Country

Now you are steering the space shuttle toward your continent. Can you land just anywhere? What part of the continent do you need to find? Most continents have many **countries**. A country is an area of land that has its own **government**.

Some countries are very large. For example, if you look at Canada and the United States on a map, you will see that they are quite large.

Other countries are much smaller. For example, if you find Cuba and El Salvador, you will see that they are small countries.

Every country has **borders** that surround it. A border is the line where one place, such as a country, ends and another begins. From space, you can't see all borders. On a map, you can see lines drawn around each country to show its borders. Sometimes mountains, rivers, and oceans help to make borders. At other times, countries have to agree on where their borders will be.

How many countries can you find on the map? Where is your country on the map?

border the line where one place, such as a state or country, ends and another begins

These are the countries of North America. Which of them do you live in?

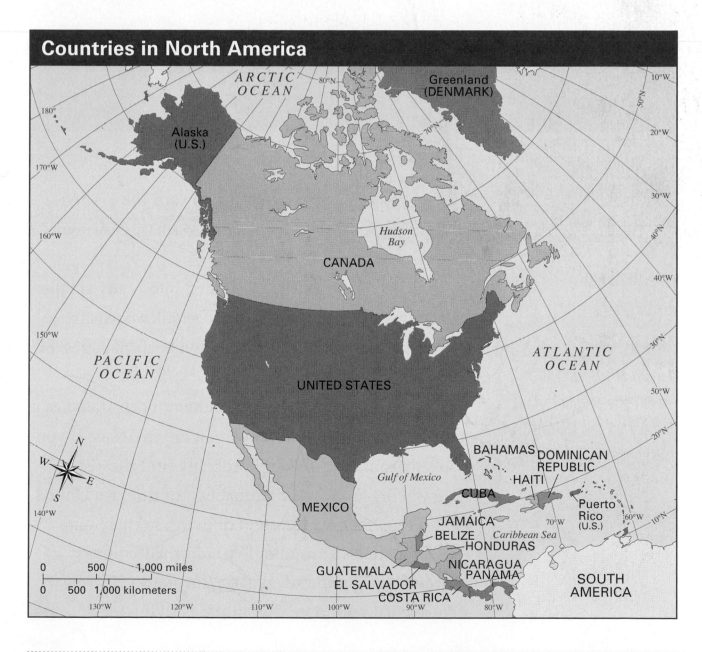

Countries in North America

ARCTIC OCEAN

Greenland (DENMARK)

Alaska (U.S.)

80°N

70°N

Hudson Bay

CANADA

PACIFIC OCEAN

ATLANTIC OCEAN

UNITED STATES

BAHAMAS

DOMINICAN REPUBLIC

HAITI

CUBA

Gulf of Mexico

Puerto Rico (U.S.)

MEXICO

JAMAICA

BELIZE

Caribbean Sea

HONDURAS

NICARAGUA

PANAMA

GUATEMALA

EL SALVADOR

COSTA RICA

SOUTH AMERICA

0   500   1,000 miles

0   500   1,000 kilometers

This image was taken with a satellite from space. Can you tell which of the 50 states it is showing?

state one of the 50 main areas with their own governments that make up the United States

4. Our Community Is in a State

The space shuttle is zooming toward the United States. The United States is a big country. How will you find the landing spot?

Most large countries are divided into many smaller parts. In the United States, these smaller parts are called **states**. These states share many similarities, but each of these states is unique.

Each state has its own government. Each state has a flag and state motto. Suppose you are in Texas. If you looked around, you would probably find the Texas flag waving. You would probably also find the United States flag. People are proud of living in their state, but they are also proud of living in their country.

Your landing spot is in a certain state. Can you figure out which state the shuttle is flying to?

Like countries, states in the United States have borders. However, you can't see many borders of states from space.

Luckily, you have a map that shows part of the United States. Each state is a different color with borders surrounding it.

Some borders are natural. For example, look at Florida's border. Only part of Florida touches the land. The rest of it sticks out into the Atlantic Ocean and the Gulf of Mexico. Because of this, most of Florida's border is made by water.

Some borders must be agreed on between states. These borders are not natural. What states are next to Florida? Alabama and Georgia share a border with Florida.

Florida, like every state, has borders. Can you spot which of Florida's borders are natural and which had to be decided on?

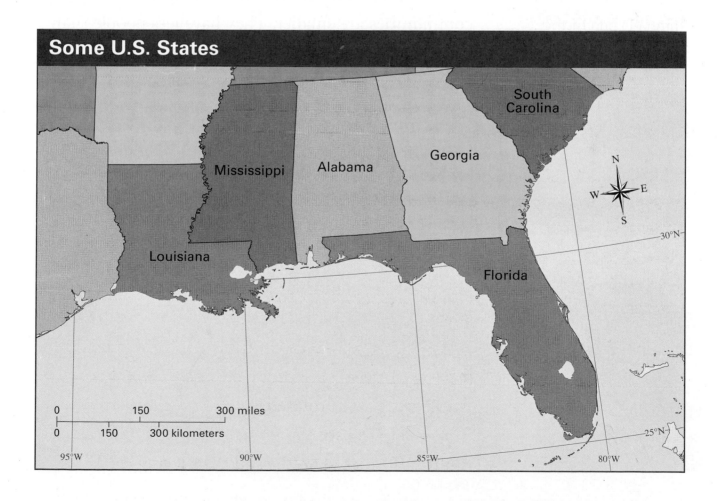

Some U.S. States

South Carolina

Mississippi Alabama Georgia

Louisiana

Florida

0   150   300 miles
0   150   300 kilometers

95°W   90°W   85°W   80°W

30°N

25°N

5. Finding Communities in a State

NASA confirms that you are headed for the state of Florida. States are made up of many communities. Communities are places where people live, work, and play. Each state has different types of communities.

Some communities are called cities. Cities are big communities with many tall buildings and people.

Look at the map of Florida. A map of a state will show places with the most people. These are usually cities. Tallahassee, Tampa, and Cape Canaveral are cities in Florida.

Tallahassee is starred on the map, which means that it is the **capital** city. The government of Florida is in Tallahassee. Florida's laws are made there.

Cities are large communities, but other communities are smaller. They have less people than cities do. We call these communities towns.

capital the city where the government of a country or state meets

Tampa is one of the biggest cities in Florida.

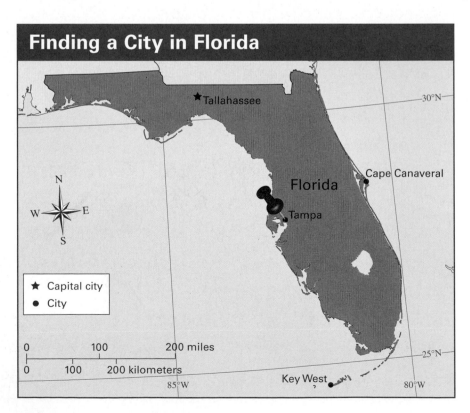

Finding a City in Florida

30°N

★Tallahassee

N
W   E
S

Florida

Cape Canaveral

Tampa

★ Capital city
● City

0   100   200 miles

0   100   200 kilometers

85°W

25°N

Key West

80°W

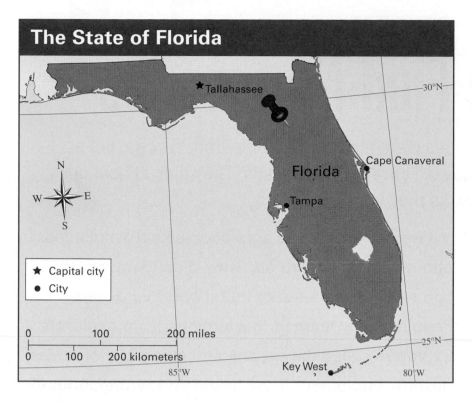

The State of Florida

Tallahassee
30°N
Florida
Cape Canaveral
Tampa

N
W   E
S

★ Capital city
● City

0   100   200 miles
0   100   200 kilometers
85°W   80°W
Key West
25°N

The pin on the map shows where the town of Micanopy is.

Most of the map does not have any city names, but this does not mean there are no communities there. There are communities all over Florida. Some of them are smaller towns. For example, one of these towns is Micanopy. It is smaller than a large city like Tampa.

The community with your landing spot is Cape Canaveral. Can you find it?

Lesson Summary

In this lesson, you learned how to tell where places are on Earth using maps. The names of hemispheres, continents, countries, and states all help us to say where a place is located. Maps show borders of places. Some borders are made by mountains and rivers, but others are decided on by people.

The space shuttle you were on was headed for a community in Florida. You saw the continent and country that Florida is part of, but you might live somewhere else. Where on Earth do *you* live?

Geography History

Explorers Find New Lands

Many of our towns and cities were started by people from Europe, but at one time, North America wasn't even on their maps. They didn't know our continent was here. How did they learn about it?

This map of the world was made in the 1500s. How is it different from world maps today?

Five hundred years ago, people knew much less about Earth than you do. They didn't know Earth had seven continents or that it had five oceans. People slowly learned these things from explorers. Explorers sailed the oceans and crossed mountains, deserts, and plains. They talked and wrote about the lands they had seen. Often, other people decided to go there, too.

Explorers Come to North America

On October 1492, three small ships tossed in the waves of the Atlantic Ocean. Many of the sailors on the ships were angry and frightened. They were trying to do something no one had done before. They were trying to sail west from Europe all the way to Asia. But they had been at sea for ten long weeks, and still there was no sign of land. The men were afraid they might never see their homes again.

The sailors' leader was an explorer named Christopher Columbus. Columbus was sure that Asia wasn't far away, so he told his sailors to be patient.

Then, on October 12, a sailor shouted, "Land!" Ahead lay a green island. That morning, Columbus excitedly led his men ashore. He always said later that he had reached Asia. But he had really come to North America.

Columbus would make three more trips to North America. He would explore many more islands in North America.

For Europeans, this was a new land, but millions of people already lived here. They were the American Indians. Now their land had been found by Europeans.

Columbus started his trip in Spain. Where did he end up?

Christopher Columbus's expedition was supposed to go to Asia, but he arrived at North America instead.

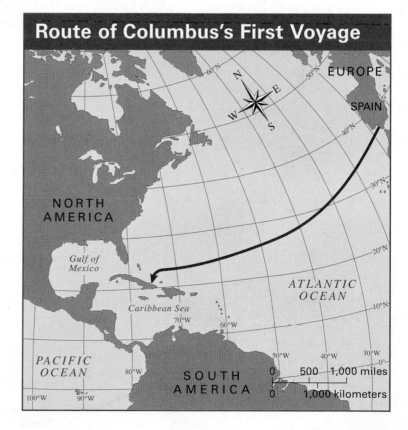

Route of Columbus's First Voyage

Explorer of
California
1542

Juan Rodríguez
CABRILLO

Juan Rodríguez Cabrillo was the first explorer to travel to California, but he died on the expedition.

Following in Columbus's footsteps, these explorers discovered new regions of North America.

Soon more explorers came. Some explored the west coast of North America. One of them was Juan Rodríguez Cabrillo (keh-BREE-yoh), who worked for Spain. In 1542, he sailed north from Mexico. He was the first European to see California.

Cabrillo never made it home. He died after he was hurt in a fight with some American Indians. But his men did get back and told what they had seen. Later, Spain sent people to live in California.

People also sailed to the east coast of North America. Some came looking for riches like fur, while, others came looking for religious freedom. Many stayed and started new communities.

Explorer	Country	Places Explored	Years
Christropher Columbus	Spain	Islands in the Caribbean Sea	1492–1504
John Cabot	England	Parts of the east coast of North America	1497–1498
Juan Ponce de León	Spain	Florida	1513–1521
Jacques Cartier	France	Parts of eastern Canada	1534–1542
Hernando de Soto	Spain	Southern parts of what is now the United States, from North Carolina to Louisiana	1539–1542
Juan Rodríguez Cabrillo	Spain	The coast of California	1542
Henry Hudson	Holland and England	Parts of eastern Canada and what is now New York State	1607–1611
Robert de la Salle	France	The Mississippi Rivier	1679–1682

Crossing North America

In 1776, people on the east coast formed a new country, which we now call the United States. Americans soon began pushing west. But they knew very little about the vast land ahead of them.

In 1804, President Thomas Jefferson sent a team of men to explore this land. Two friends, Meriwether Lewis and William Clark, led the team.

The men started their trip in the middle of the continent. They paddled up rivers, crossed grassy plains, and climbed snow-topped mountains. American Indians helped to guide and feed them along the way.

The team made it all the way to the Pacific Ocean and back. Americans were thrilled and cheered Lewis and Clark as heroes. Now people knew much more about "the West." In the years to come, many Americans would decide that the West was a fine place to live. ◆

Lewis and Clark kept notebooks, like this, during their trip.

Lewis and Clark were the first American explorers to go west of the Mississippi.

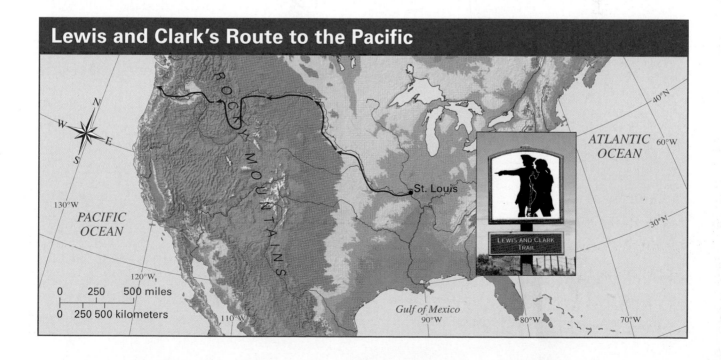

Lewis and Clark's Route to the Pacific

Finding Places in the United States

Where in the United States is our community?

Introduction

What do you notice when you look at a map of the United States? You may notice the borders of states in the country. You may notice tools that help you find places on the map. Maps help you dream about places you want to visit.

What places would you want to visit in the United States? You might want to go see the Statue of Liberty or the Golden Gate Bridge. If you want to know how to get to these places, you can use a map. Maps can tell you how far a place is from your community. They can tell you which direction to go to get to the place.

You will learn how you can find your community on a map of the United States. You will read about some famous places in this country and where you can find them on a map. You can use maps to discover where these places are compared to your community.

◀ This student is using the map to locate her community.

Geography

When you write your
address, you need to
know which state you
live in. There are 50
states in the United
States.

1. The 50 States

When you write your address, you first write the name of your street and the name of your community. Then you write the name of your state. Your state is one of many in the United States.

The United States is the country where you live. It is a country in the continent of North America. The United States has 50 states. How many of them can you name? Which state would you like to visit?

Some states are well-known because they have famous places that people like to visit. Have you heard of the Grand Canyon? It is a famous place in the state of Arizona. The Statue of Liberty is a famous landmark in the state of New York.

The states are different from each other. The weather is warmer in some states and cooler in others. Some states are close to the ocean, and others are surrounded by land. In some states, you can see plenty of farmland, but in other states, you will find busy cities instead. How would you describe the state where you live?

Each state has communities in it. What is the name of the town or city where you live? This is your community. Some states have many communities with many people living in them, but other states have fewer communities that are located farther apart.

A community may have features or landmarks that make it different from other communities. What makes your community special?

The 50 states can be very different. Some states are close to the ocean, and others are surrounded by land.

You can use a map of the United States to find different states in the country.

2. Mapping the United States

Where is your state in the United States? Do you live close or far from the ocean? Are you in the western or eastern part of the country? A map can help you answer these questions!

A map shows different places on Earth, including the United States. A map of the United States can show you the borders of the country and the 50 states.

You can figure out where your community is located in the United States by using a map. First, find the state you live in. Then, find the area where you live within the state.

Maps can also help you find other states in the country. Can you find New York, Florida, Illinois, South Dakota, Arizona, and California? You can compare their locations to your community's using the tools on a map.

Maps have a compass rose to show you the **cardinal directions,** which are north, east, south, and west. You can use the compass rose to find out if your state is to the east or west of the Mississippi River.

Maps also have symbols. The **map key** tells you what the symbols represent. For example, some maps have a star on them. The map key tells you that the star represents the U.S. capital.

A map's **scale** shows you distance. It can tell you how far places are from each other. On the map of the United States, you can use the scale to figure out how many miles South Dakota is from Arizona.

Now, you will learn about famous places in different states. You can use the map's tools to find out which direction you have to travel in to get to each place and how far places are from each other.

cardinal direction one of the four main directions: north, east, south, and west

map key a feature that explains what the symbols on a map stand for

scale a feature used to figure out distances on a map

This map shows you where the 50 states are located.

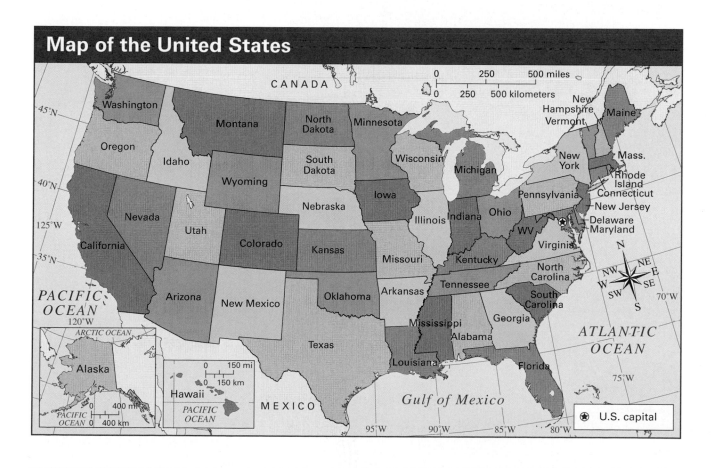

Map of the United States

3. The Statue of Liberty

Do you recognize the statue in this image? This famous statue welcomes people to the United States. It stands for freedom. It is called the Statue of Liberty.

Every year, many people visit the Statue of Liberty. If you visit this landmark, you can see the statue carrying a book and holding up a torch. The Statue of Liberty is 305 feet tall. You have to take an elevator and stairs to get to the top!

The Statue of Liberty is on a small island in New York City. This huge city is in the state of New York, which is near the Atlantic Ocean. The Atlantic Ocean touches the east coast of the United States. How far do you live from New York City?

The Statue of Liberty is a famous landmark in New York City. New York City is in the state of New York.

4. The Everglades

Have you ever seen an alligator? Would you like to meet a crocodile? You can find these and other animals in a famous place called the Everglades.

The Everglades are warm and wet. If you visit the Everglades, you will notice that the land is soggy with tall grass growing out of it. Lots of birds, snakes, crocodiles, and alligators live there, too. People visit the Everglades to camp, to see wildlife, and to fish.

The Everglades are in the state of Florida. They cover a lot of land in the southern part of this state. Florida is north and east of the Gulf of Mexico. Do you live north or south of the Everglades?

This alligator lives in the Everglades. The Everglades are a warm and wet area in the state of Florida.

The Willis Tower is the tallest building in this image. It is in Chicago, the biggest city in Illinois.

5. The Willis Tower

Many people work and live in downtown Chicago. It is a busy place with many tall buildings. Can you spot the tallest one?

The tallest building in Chicago is the Willis Tower. In fact, at 1,450 feet high, it is one of the tallest buildings in the world!

The Willis Tower opened in 1973. But at the time, it had a different name. The building was called the Sears Tower until 2009 when the name changed to the Willis Tower.

Today, many different businesses have offices there. You can also go to the observation deck near the top of the building to get a great view of the city.

This building stands at the heart of Chicago, which is in the state of Illinois. Illinois is to the east of the Mississippi River. Is your community east or west of the Mississippi River?

6. Mount Rushmore

Look at the faces carved into this mountain. Do you recognize any of them? These faces also appear on coins and dollar bills.

Mount Rushmore shows the faces of four famous U.S. presidents. The faces are 60 feet high. It took 14 years to carve them. Many people visit this landmark to take pictures with these faces every year.

Mount Rushmore is in the state of South Dakota. South Dakota is west of the Mississippi River. It is east of the Rocky Mountains. Do you live east or west of the Rocky Mountains?

The faces of four U.S. presidents are carved in Mount Rushmore in South Dakota. Can you name any of these presidents?

7. The Grand Canyon

Picture yourself at the Grand Canyon. How many different colors do you notice in the rocks? How far down is the river?

How do you think the Grand Canyon got its name? A **canyon** is a deep, narrow valley with steep sides. *Grand* means large. The Grand Canyon is certainly large! After all, it is 277 miles long and 1 mile deep.

Many people visit the Grand Canyon just to see it. Some of them hike or ride mules to get to the bottom. A river runs along the bottom of the canyon.

The Grand Canyon is in the state of Arizona. The Colorado River is in Arizona and goes through the Grand Canyon. How far do you live from the Grand Canyon?

canyon a deep, narrow valley with steep sides

The Grand Canyon is 277 miles long and 1 mile deep. This famous place is found in the state of Arizona.

8. The Golden Gate Bridge

You may recognize the Golden Gate Bridge from books or television. Where can you find this famous landmark?

The Golden Gate Bridge crosses the entrance to San Francisco Bay. The bridge opened in 1937. At the time, it had the tallest towers of any bridge in the world.

The city of San Francisco is at the south end of the bridge. San Francisco is in the state of California. People cross the bridge to get to other parts of the state. If you look to the west of the bridge, you can see the Pacific Ocean. This ocean touches the west coast of the United States. Do you live near the Pacific Ocean?

The Golden Gate Bridge is a landmark in San Francisco. San Francisco is a city in California.

Lesson Summary

If you counted them on a map, you would find that the United States has 50 states. Maps help us find states and the places within them. You could even find your state and community with a map. When you use a map to describe where a state is found, you read the cardinal directions shown on the compass rose.

Each state has many communities and landmarks for which it is known. The Statue of Liberty, the Everglades, the Willis Tower, Mount Rushmore, the Grand Canyon, and the Golden Gate Bridge are the landmarks you learned about in this lesson. Of all these places, which one would you like to visit? Why?

Civics History

Eagles, Flags, and Midnight Parades

Your community is one of many in the country. Some are east of the Rocky Mountains, and others are west. But people all over the United States feel connected. What makes us feel part of one big community?

"Let's hurry," Marisa said to her friend Jacob as she ran up the steps of her school. Marisa was excited because her school was helping to plan her town's Fourth of July celebration. Her class had chosen Jacob and Marisa to go to the planning meeting.

Marisa is from a town called Gatlinburg in the state of Tennessee. People there love to make the Fourth of July a special day.

The meeting was in the school library. As Marisa and Jacob took their seats, Ms. Lundstrom stood up. She was the school's principal.

This image shows a Fourth of July parade in 1923.

These children are marching in a recent Fourth of July parade.

"Welcome!" she said. "As you know, the Fourth of July is a very important day. On that day in 1776, the **Declaration of Independence** was approved. This great document was written by Thomas Jefferson. It said that our country would be free from the rule of Great Britain, so July fourth is the birthday of the United States. How can our town make this year's Fourth of July the best ever? Let's hear your ideas."

A boy named Amir spoke first. "We've got to have the Midnight Parade," he said. "That way we have the very first parade of the day. It's a big tradition here in Gatlinburg." A **tradition** is something that people do together year after year. A common tradition on the Fourth of July is to watch a fireworks show.

Declaration of Independence a document that said that the United States is free from the rule of Great Britain

tradition something that people do together year after year

"But how can we make the parade special?" Ms. Lundstrom asked.

"We could have giant balloons that are shaped like bald eagles," Marisa said.

Everyone liked that idea because the bald eagle is the national bird. It is a **symbol** of courage and freedom. A symbol is something that stands for an idea.

Then Tina spoke. "There should be a band that plays patriotic songs while leading the parade," she said.

"The band should play 'The Star-Spangled Banner,'" Marisa added. "It's the national anthem."

"We learned some other good songs," Amir said. "I like 'You're a Grand Old Flag' and the 'Liberty Bell March.'"

"That's a great idea!" said Mrs. Lundstrom. "These songs tell about American symbols. The flag stands for our strength and for everything that makes us one country."

People have been singing this song about the flag for more than 100 years. *Emblem* means symbol. In the song, what is the flag a symbol of?

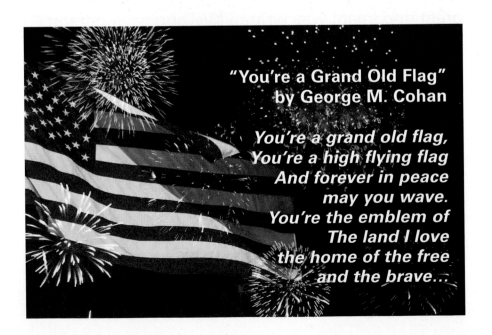

"You're a Grand Old Flag"
by George M. Cohan

You're a grand old flag,
You're a high flying flag
And forever in peace
may you wave.
You're the emblem of
The land I love
the home of the free
and the brave...

The Liberty Bell has had a crack in it since 1846. No one has rung it since then.

"We should give flags to everyone," said Tina. "Every country has its own flag. The American flag is one of the most important symbols for our country."

"Everyone, make sure to wear red, white, and blue!" said Amir. "Those are the colors on our flag and also are our country's colors. It is a good way to show support of the United States."

"Ms. Lundstrom, what does the Liberty Bell stand for?" asked Jacob.

"It stands for freedom," responded Ms. Lundstrom.

"I saw it once in the city of Philadelphia," Marisa said. "People rang it in 1776 when they were going to read the Declaration of Independence out loud. They wanted everyone to come and hear it being read."

Many people visit the Lincoln Memorial each year in Washington, D.C. A statue of Abraham Lincoln, the 16th president of the United States, sits inside the building.

The Washington Monument in Washington, D.C., honors President George Washington.

"We could have somebody dress up as the Statue of Liberty," Tina said. "The statue welcomed people who come to America from other countries."

"The Statue of Liberty is a great symbol," said Ms. Lundstrom. "It represents freedom and opportunity."

"Our country has many other symbols," continued Ms. Lundstrom. "The Washington Monument is one. It is in Washington, D.C., and built in honor of our first president, George Washington."

"I saw it when I visited Washington, D.C.," said Tina. "There are a lot of symbols there because it is our country's capital."

"Yes, there are," Amir agreed. "It has the Lincoln Memorial, which honors President Abraham Lincoln, and other memorials to remember famous wars. The memorials for the Vietnam War and World War II are in Washington, D.C."

"I have another idea for the parade," Tina said. "Let's set up a booth to tell about our history. Someone can read the Declaration, and we can show a copy of the Constitution. Then people can see the words that helped form our government."

"And we could have pictures of the U.S. Capitol building," Jacob said. "It's also in Washington, D.C., and people write our laws there."

The Fourth of July plan was sounding better and better. Marisa smiled as she thought about herself marching down the street at midnight. She could even hear the band playing! ◆

The U.S. Capitol building in Washington, D.C., is where our government makes laws for our country.

Geography and the Way We Live

How does geography affect our community?

Introduction

What do you think of when you hear the word *geography*? If you thought of maps and globes, you're right. People use geography skills to help them find places on a map. But geography isn't just about where places are. It's also about what different places are like.

Look at this image of Boulder, Colorado. You can see how the land is shaped. Homes and buildings are located down in the valley. Tall mountains surround the valley. They are covered with trees and even snow. These things are all part of the area's geography.

In this lesson, you'll read about the geography of four places in the United States. You'll learn what makes these places different from one another and how those differences affect the way people live in their community.

> **Social Studies Vocabulary**
>
> adapt
> climate
> conservation
> natural hazard
> natural resource
> physical feature
> physical geography
> pollution
> region

◀ This photograph of Boulder, Colorado, was taken from above. What do you notice about the shape of the land?

Geography

1. What Is Geography?

If you went for a bus ride near your community, what would you see? Would you see tall mountains or flat plains? Would you see a lake or a river? These landforms and bodies of water are all examples of **physical features** of Earth's surface. Physical features are made by nature, not by people. They are part of the **physical geography** of the area where you live.

The geography of a place includes other things, too. For example, **climate** is a part of physical geography. Climate means what the weather in a place is like, measured over time.

Different places often have different climates. Some places get lots of rain, while others hardly ever see a cloud. Some places are icy cold in winter and boiling hot in summer. Others have mild weather almost all year round.

physical feature
a natural feature of Earth's surface, such as a mountain, plain, lake, or river

physical geography
the physical features, climate, and natural resources of a place

climate the weather in a place, measured over time

This illustration shows different landforms and bodies of water found on Earth. These are examples of physical features.

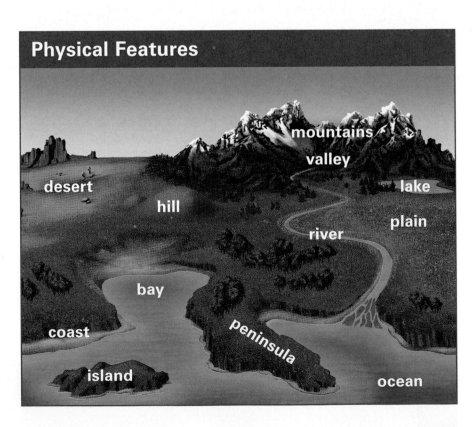

Physical Features

mountains
valley
lake
desert
plain
hill
river
bay
peninsula
coast
island
ocean

The state of Hawaii is made of many islands. These islands are created by volcanoes.

People use many things from nature in their daily lives. These things are examples of **natural resources**. People use wood from trees to build houses, and they use land and water to grow food. These resources are also part of physical geography. What are some of the natural resources near your community?

Natural hazards play an important role in shaping Earth's geography. For example, earthquakes can knock down trees and change the shape of the land. Volcanoes can create islands. Some places have climates that cause more natural hazards like hurricanes and tornadoes. Natural hazards can change Earth's surface quickly. They are also extremely dangerous.

natural resource
a useful item that comes from nature, such as wood from trees

natural hazard
a force of nature that shapes Earth

People in Anchorage dress warmly because of the cold.

adapt to change ways of living to fit an environment

2. Adapting to Geography

Different kinds of physical geography have their own challenges. Water can be hard to find in areas with dry climates. Mountains can make it hard for people to get from place to place.

People must **adapt** to the physical geography around them. Adaptation happens over time as people learn more about their surroundings.

In Anchorage, Alaska, it usually snows over 70 inches each year. How have the people who live here adapted to the big snowfalls?

People in Anchorage wear warm clothes to protect themselves from low temperatures. They shovel the sidewalks so that people can go outside safely. People in Anchorage have cars that they can drive in the snow.

When people settle in an area, they affect their surroundings. Some of these effects are bad. Other effects are good.

Sometimes, people pollute the area around them. **Pollution** is a bad effect. Trash can enter rivers and wash up onto shores.

Overusing natural resources is another bad effect. People use natural resources, such as trees, to build homes. But if they use too many trees, they can clear large sections of forests where many plants and animals live.

People can protect the environment by using natural resources wisely. **Conservation** is a good effect. If people use fewer trees to build homes, then less land would be cleared. This would protect the plants and animals that live in that area.

pollution anything that makes air, water, or soil dirty or unsafe

conservation the careful use of natural resources

This photograph of the Mississippi River shows waste that has entered the water.

This is an overhead view of Roseburg, Oregon. How do you think this picture was taken?

region an area with certain common features that set it apart from other areas

3. The Geography of Roseburg, Oregon

Geography has a lot to do with how we live. To see why this is so, let's look at four cities. We'll start with Roseburg, Oregon.

Oregon is in the Northwest **region** of the United States. A region is an area with certain features in common. The Northwest has lots of mountains, trees, and rivers.

People in Roseburg know all about these physical features. Roseburg is in a valley of the Cascade Mountains. Tall trees cover the mountains, and a big river runs through the city. Many people go fishing in the river.

The climate in Roseburg is gentle and mild, and rarely gets very cold or very hot. Winters are cool and rainy, while summers are warm and dry.

Roseburg's climate helps plants and trees grow. Forests are the most important natural resource in Roseburg. People work in lumber mills, cutting down trees and sending the lumber to other places. (Lumber is wood that has been cut from trees.)

Lumber mills have been in Roseburg for many years. Some people make sure that more trees are planted to replace those that are cut down. Why do you think they do this?

Logs are stacked at a lumber mill before they are shipped.

This is a view of Las Cruces, New Mexico.

4. The Geography of Las Cruces, New Mexico

The city of Las Cruces (lahs-CROO-says) is in New Mexico. This state is in the Southwest region of the United States. This is a region of sandy deserts and rugged mountains.

The geography of Las Cruces has three important physical features. First, Las Cruces is in the middle of a desert. Second, there are mountains nearby. Third, the city was built next to a river. The river is called the Rio Grande, which means "great river" in Spanish.

Las Cruces has a desert climate, so the weather is usually hot and dry. There is very little rain. In the summer, it is very hot. Temperatures can climb over 100 degrees. To stay cool, some homes in the city are built from a clay brick called *adobe*. Adobe keeps homes cool in the summer and warm in the winter.

Can you guess what the most important natural resource in Las Cruces is? It's water. Deserts have very little water. But people, animals, and plants all need water to live. The people in Las Cruces use their water wisely and are careful not to waste it. Where does the water come from?

The desert around Las Cruces is very dry.

These boats are docked in Gloucester, Massachusetts. The ocean is an important physical feature in Gloucester.

5. The Geography of Gloucester, Massachusetts

The city of Gloucester (GLAWS-ter) is in Massachusetts. This state is in the Northeast region of the United States. The Atlantic Ocean is to the east of this region.

The ocean is the most important physical feature near Gloucester. In fact, the city has ocean water on three sides.

People in Gloucester need lots of different clothes. The weather there changes from season to season. Summers are warm and sunny. Winters are cold and snowy. Spring and fall are cool and rainy.

The weather around Gloucester even changes from day to day. People in this part of the country say, "If you don't like the weather, wait five minutes and it will change."

Fish and other seafood are the most important natural resources in Gloucester. Since the city is close to the water, many people fish for a living. They spend many days at sea on fishing boats and then sell the fish they have caught. Other people dig for clams or trap lobsters. How have the people in Gloucester adapted to living in this area?

The weather in Gloucester can change at any moment.

Galveston is an island city. It sits off the east coast of Texas.

6. The Geography of Galveston, Texas

The city of Galveston is in the state of Texas. Texas is located in the Southwest region of the United States.

Galveston sits on an island off the coast of the Texas mainland. It is surrounded by the Gulf of Mexico. The Gulf is the most important physical feature of Galveston. Fish and crab are two key natural resources that are found in the Gulf.

Since Galveston is very close to a body of water and located closer to the equator, it gets humid there. Humidity makes the air feel wet and heavy. Texas also gets very hot in the summers. Most people have air conditioning to help cool down. However, the winters in Galveston are mild.

Since Galveston is on the coast, it is in danger of being hit by hurricanes. Hurricanes are storms that start in the ocean and often get bigger as they move toward land. Many homes in Galveston are built on stilts, or poles, to protect them from floods and winds.

But some hurricanes can do a lot of harm. In 2008, Galveston was struck by Hurricane Ike. The city became blanketed in water. The hurricane tore trees down and washed away much of Galveston's coastline. Many buildings and cars were damaged, too.

Galveston has worked hard to recover from Hurricane Ike. Natural hazards can create long-lasting damage in a short amount of time.

Natural hazards such as hurricanes can change a place's physical geography. Hurricane Ike greatly affected the city of Galveston.

Lesson Summary

In this lesson, you learned about different physical features on Earth's surface. People in a community adapt to their environment. You also learned about four cities with different physical features, climate, and resources. All these things are part of their geography. You learned about natural hazards and how they shape the Earth. Natural hazards are very dangerous.

What is the geography like where you live? Do you think any of it has been shaped by hazards? Can you think of any natural resources in your area?

Telling Stories with Maps

Your community may be near a lake or a desert. The land in and around your community may be flat or hilly. You might have natural resources nearby, such as trees or fish. Maps can show all these things, but how do maps get made?

Cartographers make all different kinds of maps. This digital map can be viewed on an electronic device.

My name is Belinda, and I tell stories about places. Because I'm a cartographer, I use maps instead of words. Cartographer is a fancy name for a person who makes maps.

I can tell many kinds of stories with my maps. How do I decide what story to tell? The answer depends on two things: the purpose of the map and who is going to be reading it.

The Great Lakes Region

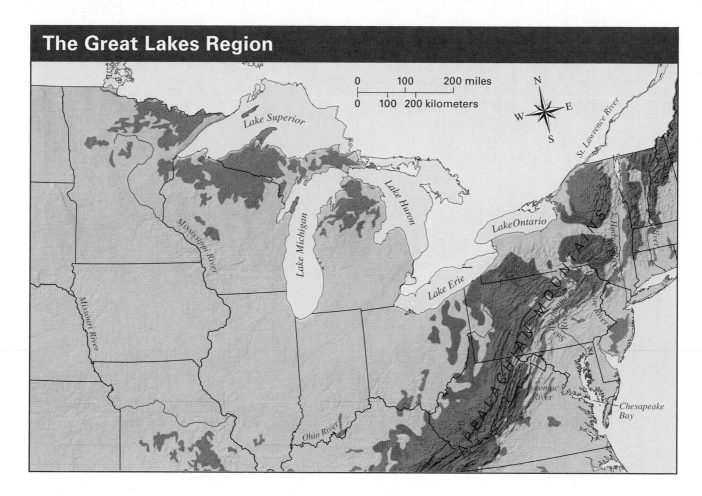

Let's say that the map's purpose is to show the main physical features of the Great Lakes region of the United States. Students like you will study the map to learn about these features.

As a cartographer, my job is to create a map that shows you these things. I need to show features like rivers, lakes, and mountains. But on this map, I won't show lots of other things, like roads and cities. They would be important on a different kind of map, but not this one. On this map, I want people to look just at physical features.

My first step is making sure I have gathered all the necessary information. I have to be sure that I include important features on my map and put them in the correct locations.

This is a map of the Great Lakes Region. It shows the physical features of the area.

This is an aerial photo of the Great Lakes region.

How I Gather Information

Where do I get my information? I read books and also study other maps.

Sometimes I use aerial photographs, which are photos taken from a plane. I can put several of these photographs together to see a large area.

I can also look at photographs taken from space. Space shuttles and satellites (spacecraft that go around Earth) carry the cameras into space so they can be used. Photographs taken from space are very useful for showing Earth's physical features.

Next, I have to choose a type of map to draw on. Such a map is called a base map. This time, I will use a base map that shows the outline of the entire United States. The base map will also show state borders. These lines will help you see where different features are.

How I Put Information on a Map

The mainland of the United States is about 3,000 miles wide. I have to show that huge area in a space that will fit in a book, while also squeezing in Alaska and Hawaii. So I need to figure out how many miles each inch of my map will stand for. Then I draw a scale on the map, which helps measure the distances between places. I also draw a compass rose so you can tell directions.

Next, I select colors for the map, choosing ones that help you see things quickly and easily. For instance, I might use shades of green for most land areas. But I might use brown for mountains and other high places.

The physical features of the United States are shown on this map.

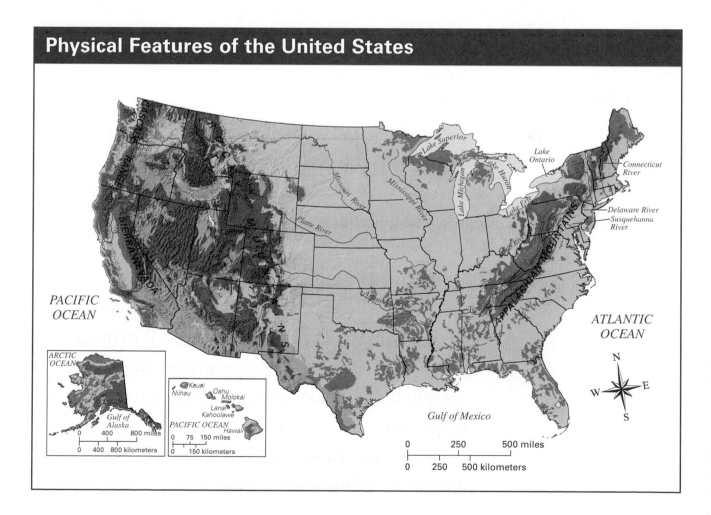

Physical Features of the United States

Physical Features Map with Grid

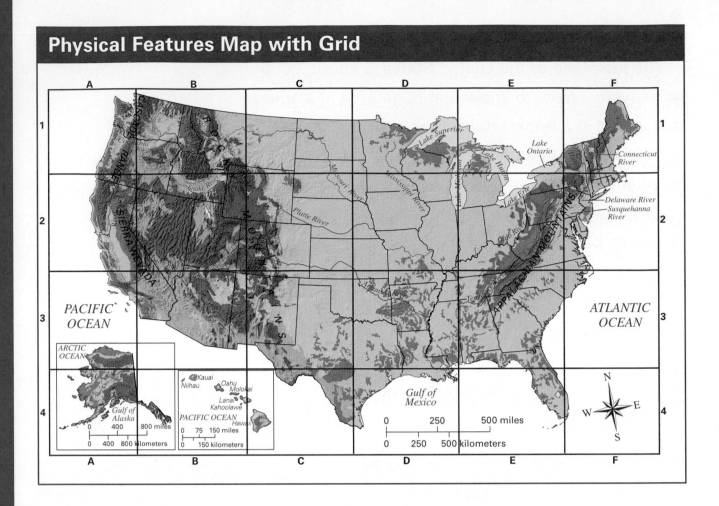

This physical features map of the United States uses a grid.

Simple grids like this one make it easier to locate places on a map.

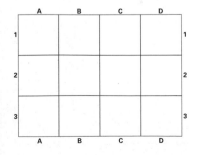

How I Help You Locate Features

As a cartographer, I want you to be able to tell the location of places on the map. One way to do this is to draw a grid on the map. A grid is made up of squares in columns and rows, like the squares in a game of tic-tac-toe.

I give each column a letter and each row a number so we can name every square on the grid. For example, find the column labeled D in the grid to the left, then move a finger straight down this column to the second row. You have found the square D2.

We can use grids like this one to say exactly where a place is. In which square can you find Lake Erie?

How I Make a Special-purpose Map

Sometimes maps tell a story about a single topic. This kind of map is called a **special-purpose map**.

In the Northwest, fish called salmon are an important resource. Many people make a living by catching and selling salmon. But in some places, salmon are dying out. Maps can help us keep track of the salmon so we can protect this resource.

I can make a special-purpose map to show where the salmon are. First, I gather facts about which lakes and streams have salmon. Then, I use symbols to show this information on a map. I put a key, or legend, on the map to tell what the symbols mean.

I love telling stories with maps, because I know that my maps help people learn more about their world. ◆

special-purpose map a map that shows information about a single topic

Lakes and streams where salmon live are shown on this special-purpose map.

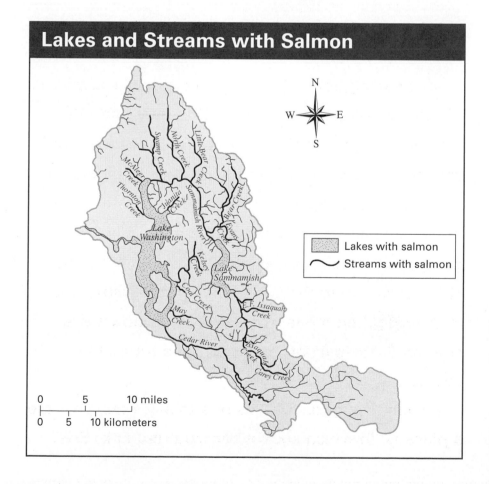

Lakes and Streams with Salmon

Lakes with salmon
Streams with salmon

0   5   10 miles
0   5   10 kilometers

Settling in the United States

How do people become part of our country?

Introduction

People from many different places live in the United States. But how did we all get here? American Indians have lived here for thousands of years. But many groups of people have come much more recently to the United States.

Europeans began to come here about 500 years ago. Since then, people have come from many different countries. Today, people from all over the world come to the United States.

In this lesson, you will read about some of these people. You will find out why and how they came here to live. You will discover when and where these people settled. You will learn about the challenges they faced when they arrived. Finally, you will explore how these people became part of our country.

◀ Immigrants arrive at Ellis Island, New York. Why did these people come to the United States?

 Civics Economics Geography History

This engraving shows Irish immigrants on a ship bound for the United States. Many left Ireland because of the disease that killed potato plants.

immigrant a person who comes from another place to live in a country

1. Why Immigrants Come to the United States

When people move to another country to live, they are called **immigrants**. Immigrants have come to the United States for many reasons. Sometimes they may need to get away from problems. There might be wars or unfair laws where they live. Sometimes there are too many people in a place without enough jobs or food for everyone.

Once, in Ireland, a disease started to kill all the potato plants in the country. Potatoes were an important food there. When the plants died, people began to starve. Many families left their homes and moved to the United States.

After the Irish, many immigrants from other countries fled to the United States. Millions of Italians came to the United States to escape poverty. Jewish immigrants from Eastern Europe came to evade unfair treatment. And Mexicans came to avoid a bloody civil war.

But people don't move here just to escape problems. Often they simply want a chance for a better life. That is one reason our country grew quickly in the 1800s.

Many people came from Europe to get good jobs or to start farms. When gold was discovered in California, people came rushing to the gold fields from all over the world. Only a few of them got rich, but many stayed anyway. Can you think of some reasons why people might want to come to the United States today?

Thousands of people rushed to the gold fields in California hoping to make a fortune.

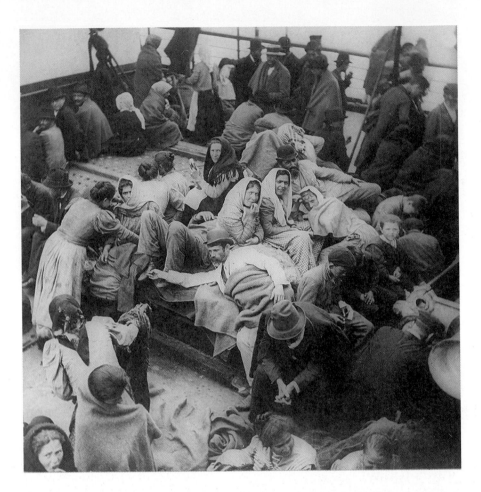

Immigrants traveled to America by ship. Filthy toilets sometimes made the ship smell so bad that passengers crowded onto the main deck for fresh air.

2. How Immigrants Come to the United States

Getting to the United States is often very hard for immigrants. In the past, people came from Asia and Europe on crowded ships. These people included the Irish, the Jews, and the Chinese.

Often, the conditions on the ships were awful. The ships were unsanitary and overcrowded with passengers. A ship might take weeks crossing the ocean. But not all immigrants traveled to the United States by sea. People from Mexico and other places sometimes walked hundreds of miles.

Things weren't easy after the trip was over, either. Government officials tested new immigrants to see if they were healthy. If they were sick, they could be sent home.

Immigrants also had to answer a lot of questions. They had to say where they were going to stay and show how they were going to make a living. Sometimes they didn't have good answers and were turned away. But millions were allowed to stay.

Today, getting to the United States is a lot easier because of airplanes. But it is even harder to stay.

Before coming to the United States, immigrants must get permission to stay here. They have to hire lawyers and fill out lots of papers. The process is expensive and can take years. Sometimes whole families save money so just one person can immigrate. Often, they hope that the rest of the family can come later on.

Immigrants had to show they were healthy. These immigrants are having their eyes checked for disease.

3. Settling in the United States

People from all over the world have immigrated to the United States. But they did not all come at the same time, and they did not all settle in the same place.

About 170 years ago, many immigrants came to the United States from Ireland and Germany. They crossed the Atlantic Ocean and arrived on the east coast of the United States.

There were a lot of jobs available in northeastern cities, and the Irish tended to settle in cities such as New York City, Boston, and Philadelphia. Germans, who usually had more money than the Irish, often moved west and became farmers.

After the Irish and Germans first came, an even greater wave of immigrants arrived. This time most of the immigrants were coming from Southern and Eastern Europe.

Immigrants often settled in northeastern cities where they found jobs. Many Italian immigrants lived in "Little Italys" such as this one in New York City.

Immigrants from the same country often settled in the same neighborhoods. Italians found work in New York City, where they settled their own neighborhoods called "Little Italys." Jewish immigrants flocked to the Lower East Side of New York City, where many made clothes for a living.

Chinese immigrants crossed the Pacific Ocean and arrived on the West Coast. They came to California seeking gold. They often settled in neighborhoods like Chinatown in San Francisco.

A little over a century ago, many Mexicans immigrated to California and the Southwest. Many worked on farms or railroads.

Today, most immigrants come from Asia and Latin America. Are there immigrants living in your community? Where are they from?

Many Chinese immigrants settled in California city neighborhoods, such as Chinatown in San Francisco.

Immigrants often work long hours in difficult jobs.

discriminate to treat people unfairly because they belong to a different group

4. Life for Immigrants in the United States

Many immigrants come to the United States for a better future, but starting life in a new country can be hard. Sometimes people **discriminate** against immigrants. To discriminate means to treat people unfairly because they belong to a different group.

When groups of immigrants first arrived, they needed jobs and housing. But many hospitals did not hire Jewish doctors, and housing was closed to Chinese immigrants in many areas. Many Italians were treated like criminals because a few Italians had become famous criminals. And Mexican immigrants were paid very low wages.

Immigrants today face challenges, too. Some immigrants have to take jobs that no one else wants. These jobs can be dangerous. Often they don't pay much money. Many immigrants work long hours to earn the money they need.

Immigrants also find good things about life here. They may have more freedom than they had before. If they work hard, they may get better jobs. Then they and their children can have even better lives in the United States.

Some immigrants are famous in our country. Albert Einstein, an award-winning scientist, came here from Germany. Einstein was a Jew, and at the time, Germany was a dangerous place for Jews to live. He came to our country for protection.

Ileana Ros-Lehtinen (ih-lee-AH-nah rahs-LAY-tih-nin) is a member of the U.S. House of Representatives. She came from Cuba. In 1989, Ros-Lehtinen became the first Latina elected to Congress.

Albert Einstein (left) and Ileana Ros-Lehtinen (right) both immigrated to the United States. Immigrants often find more opportunities in this country than at home.

Immigrants become American citizens in ceremonies like this one. How do immigrants become part of our country?

citizen a person who has the right to live in a certain place

5. Becoming a U.S. Citizen

Suppose you are an immigrant to the United States. You've traveled all the way here for a better life. You want to live in the United States for the rest of your life. But first, you must become a U.S. citizen.

A **citizen** is a person who has the right to live in a certain place. So, a U.S. citizen is a person who has the right to live in the United States. There are two ways to become a U.S. citizen: by birth or through law.

To become a U.S. citizen at birth, you must be born in the United States or have parents who are U.S. citizens. But most immigrants do not meet these standards. They are not born in the United States, and their parents are usually not U.S. citizens. So, most immigrants must become citizens through law.

Becoming a citizen through law can take years. To qualify, you must be 18 or older. You have to live in the United States for at least five years. You need to apply and take a test on American history and the English language. Only after you pass the test will you become a U.S. citizen. An immigrant can also qualify to apply for citizenship by marrying a U.S. citizen or joining the military.

Not all immigrants become U.S. citizens. About half of the immigrants in the United States are now U.S. citizens. Those immigrants can now call America home.

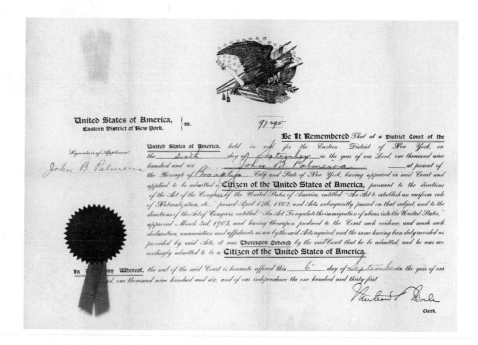

This is a certificate making an immigrant from Portugal a U.S. citizen. It took him years to get it.

Lesson Summary

Immigrants come to the United States for many reasons. Some want to get away from problems. Others hope for a good job or more freedom. After arriving here, immigrants often settle where they can find jobs. They also settle in places where other immigrants from the same country live.

Being an immigrant can be hard. Immigrants may face discrimination. It can take a long time for them to adjust to a new home. But many people around the world believe coming to the United States is their best chance for a better life.

Economics Geography History

One Immigrant's Story

Each year, thousands of people choose to move to the United States. This is the story of one immigrant and her family. What was it like for a young girl to become part of our country?

Esperanza was born in Mexico. As a young girl, she lived in a very small village. The people in her village were very poor, and many had built their own houses out of sticks. Esperanza's father was good at building things, and he made their house out of cement blocks.

Most of Esperanza's neighbors were *campesinos*, or poor farmers. The people in her village worked in the fields, and they had just enough food to live on.

The United States seemed very far away. It was on the other side of deserts and mountains. Esperanza never dreamed that she would leave her home and live there one day. Her home was in Mexico.

Many of Esperanza's neighbors lived in houses like these.

Esperanza's parents had five children. She had three sisters and one brother. Esperanza's father had to work in the fields like many of her neighbors, and her family did not have very much money. When the work in one field was done, her father would move to another one.

People who move from place to place to get work are called **migrant workers**. Often, migrant workers are not paid very much. It was hard for Esperanza's father to earn enough money for his big family.

Still, Esperanza liked many things about her life. She had friends, and she knew everyone in her village. Esperanza even liked her school, which was in a large town miles from her village. Most of all, she liked living near her grandparents.

But her father wanted to give his children a better life. He needed to decide how to do this.

Usually, migrant workers get little pay for their work.

migrant worker
someone who moves from place to place to get work

A Big Decision

Esperanza's father faced a big decision. Should he continue working as a migrant worker in Mexico? Or should he try to find a better job in the United States?

You have different ways of making big decisions. One way is to think about what will change if you make a certain choice. You can start with the benefits, or good things, that you think will happen.

Esperanza's father thought that moving to the United States would have many benefits. He could get a better job and earn more money for his family.

He also believed that schools in the United States were better than the schools in Mexico. If they moved to the United States, his children would get a better education.

When Esperanza was young, her family moved to the town of El Paso, Texas.

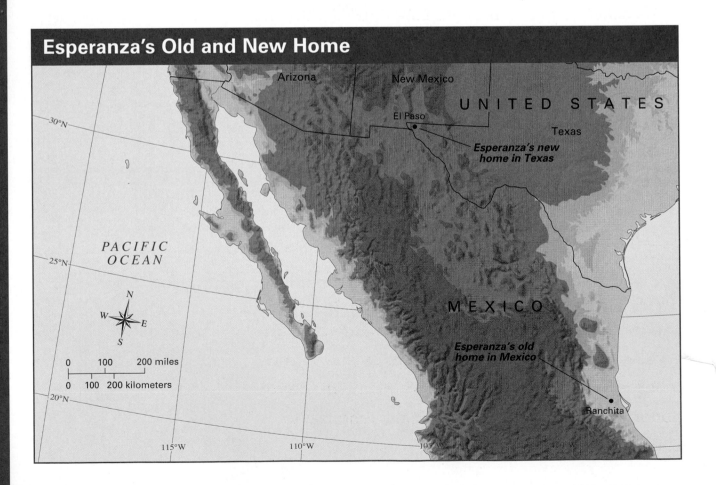

Esperanza's Old and New Home

Arizona
New Mexico
UNITED STATES
El Paso
Texas
Esperanza's new home in Texas
30°N
PACIFIC OCEAN
25°N
N
W   E
S
MEXICO
Esperanza's old home in Mexico
0   100   200 miles
0   100   200 kilometers
20°N
Ranchita
115°W   110°W

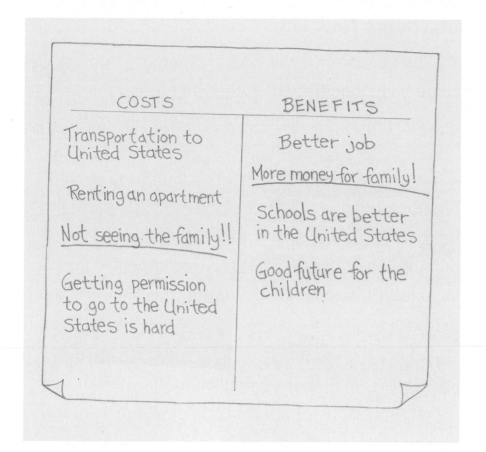

COSTS

Transportation to United States

Renting an apartment

Not seeing the family!!

Getting permission to go to the United States is hard

BENEFITS

Better job

More money for family!

Schools are better in the United States

Good future for the children

People often have to make big decisions. It can help to write down costs and benefits.

Most decisions also have costs. For instance, Esperanza's father would need money to move to the United States. It would also take time for him to get permission from the United States to work there.

There was another kind of cost, too. Her father would have to give up some things if he moved. He did not have enough money to bring Esperanza or the rest of his family right away. That meant that he would have to give up seeing his wife and children for a while. He would also have to give up the money he was making as a farmworker.

Esperanza's father thought about all the benefits and costs. He tried to decide which ones were the most important. Then he made up his mind. He said goodbye to his family and began the long trip to El Paso, a city in Texas.

Starting a New Life

When Esperanza was a little older, her family came back together. Her father had asked the government to allow him to bring the rest of his family to the United States.

Esperanza was happy that her family was back together, but she missed her village. She was a little worried, too. Esperanza had felt at home in Mexico, but she did not know what life would be like for her in Texas. El Paso was much larger than her village in Mexico.

At first, it was hard to make friends because Esperanza did not speak English. It was hard for her to talk with some of her classmates. English was also hard to learn. She spent a lot of time in the library reading books in English. She also watched TV shows. These shows gave her more practice with English, and they also helped her learn about American life.

People immigrate to states like Texas to find a better life.

Building a Community

In El Paso, Esperanza's family only knew a few people. She was glad that she had neighbors who were Mexican, too. They spoke Spanish like her, so she could easily understand them. Soon, they felt like family to her.

As time passed, Esperanza began to feel more at home in El Paso. She found that many people were immigrants like her. These immigrants worked together to help each other.

The man who owned the grocery store that her family shopped at was from Mexico, too. He helped his fellow immigrants in any way he could. He would give jobs to people who needed work or even give food or money to families that did not have enough.

The people in El Paso had created a community. This community helped protect and support people who had come from Mexico.

El Paso, Texas, is a lot larger than the village in Mexico where Esperanza grew up.

Esperanza's father helped people build things and hired other people to help him.

Helping Other Immigrants

In the United States, Esperanza's father worked in construction. He helped design and create new buildings. At first, he helped build new things around El Paso. Many people liked the work he did. Then he began to travel to other states, like Arizona and New Mexico, to build new things there as well.

Soon, he was able to start his own construction business. As his business grew, he was able to hire people to help him. Some of the people he hired were immigrants. As they worked together, her father helped these new immigrants learn English so that they could work better in their communities.

Esperanza's father continued to work hard in his business. Her father saved up enough money so that she and her brothers and sisters could go to college.

With the support of her community in El Paso, Esperanza went to college and chose to become a teacher. She also worked hard and became a citizen of the United States. Soon, she found a job in California as a teacher.

Today, many of her students in California are immigrants. They come from all over the world. Like Esperanza, many of these students did not know English when they moved here. She remembers how hard it was to learn, so she helps these immigrants learn the language.

Esperanza is proud of her students, and she wants to help them get used to their new country. She wants to help them form a community that will help them succeed, like her community did for her. ◆

Esperanza worked hard as a teacher and helped many students learn English.

Diversity in the United States

What different groups of people make up our culture?

Introduction

Imagine living in a big city like New York. If you walk down the street, you'll see many types of restaurants. You might hear people speaking different languages and see people playing different games. Many of these things come from different cultures.

A culture is a way of life that a group of people shares. The people in a group have things in common. They may be from the same country or practice the same religion. These people have a certain culture. A group may have languages, foods, music, and games that are part of their culture.

Our country is a very diverse place. Diverse means made up of different groups of people or cultures. In this lesson, you will explore some of the things that different cultures bring to our nation and communities.

◄ These Americans are celebrating Thanksgiving during a parade in New York City.

Geography

Social Studies Vocabulary

culture
diverse

European immigrants pack a ship headed for the United States. Why would these people want to come to the United States?

1. Our Community Shares Different Cultures

If you go to New York City, you may notice many different groups of people. You may also notice different food, music, and languages. Why is this place so **diverse**?

People came to this country from all over the world. They came to better their lives or to get away from problems. Many sailed from Europe to places like New York City. Others were forced to come from Africa as slaves.

People came from other countries, too. Some sailed from Asia to the West Coast. Others traveled north from Mexico and South America.

The places that immigrants come from have different ways of life, or **cultures**. Different things make up culture. A culture shares certain food, languages, holidays, and traditions. When immigrants arrive in the United States, they bring parts of their culture with them. Bits and pieces of these cultures find their way into American culture. This makes our country diverse.

There are many different types of food, languages, holidays, and traditions in American culture because so many different groups came to this country. The food we eat comes from different places. So do the games we play and the music we listen to. Even some holidays Americans celebrate come from different cultures.

You may have friends from all types of cultures. People from different cultures may go to the same school as you. They may celebrate some of the same holidays as you. The way they live and the way you live help make up American culture.

In the United States, people come from different countries, but they share parts of their cultures with each other. What foods, languages, holidays, and traditions make up our culture?

Students in class with you may come from many different cultural backgrounds.

Bagels, a very popular food in the United States, come from Jewish culture.

2. Our Community Shares Different Foods

You're walking down a street in New York. Each restaurant you pass is different. One is Italian, and the next one is Chinese.

Food is an important part of any culture. When people move to a new place, they often keep making the foods they are used to eating. Many communities have people from different cultures, so we also have many kinds of foods.

Many popular foods come from Europe. Do you like gingerbread? Europeans have made it for hundreds of years. Spaghetti comes from the Italian culture, and bagels come from the Jewish culture in Europe.

Have you ever tasted borscht? It is a soup made from beets. Borscht comes from the Russian culture. How about a gyro (YEE-roh)? A gyro is a sandwich made with roasted meat and pita bread. It comes from the Greek culture.

People often eat food that is from a culture other their own. In this Italian restaurant in New York City, many of the people eating may not have an Italian background.

Some restaurants in the United States serve a Vietnamese dish called pho, which is a soup of noodles and meat.

Asian Americans also have brought their foods to the United States. Do you like Japanese sushi? Or Chinese chow mein (chow-MAYN)? What about pho? Pho is a soup of noodles and meat. It comes from the country of Vietnam. Have you ever had tandoori chicken? This spicy dish comes from India.

Many popular foods come from Latin American cultures. These are the cultures of Mexico, Central America, and South America. For instance, you may like tacos and tamales (tuh-MAH-leez). They come from the Mexican culture.

African Americans share other foods. Hoppin' John is a stew of pork, rice, and black-eyed peas.

What are some of the foods that people eat where you live? What cultures do these foods come from?

3. Our Community Shares Different Languages

Most people in the United States speak English. But many of us also use other languages. If you visit neighborhoods across the country, you may see signs in Chinese or hear people speak Spanish.

Many Americans from Arab families live in Dearborn, Michigan. You may see Arabic signs or hear the Arabic language there. In some California neighborhoods, you may hear people speak Vietnamese. Immigrants from Vietnam settled in these places. Millions of Latinos live in Texas and throughout the country. They may speak Spanish in their homes and with friends.

You probably speak some of these languages, even if you don't know it! That's because we get many English words from other languages. *Algebra* comes from Arabic. *Guitar* and *mosquito* are from Spanish. The names of many places also come from Spanish. *Florida* comes from the Spanish word meaning flowers.

This neighborhood has street signs in two languages, English and Chinese.

We get words from many other languages, too. For example, the word *banana* is a West African word. The word *cookie* comes from Dutch. But the word *pretzel* is a German word.

Long before Europeans came to our land, many American Indian groups lived here. They had hundreds of languages. People still speak some of these languages today, such as Navajo and Cherokee. Some English words and names come from these languages, too. *Skunk* is one example, and another is *Kentucky*.

What about where you live? What are some languages that you hear in your community?

Some stores sell newspapers in many languages.

These dancers are part of a Cinco de Mayo celebration. Cinco de Mayo is a holiday that comes from Mexican culture.

4. Our Community Shares Different Holidays

Do you like holidays? Holidays are more than days when we don't have to go to school or work. They are days when we honor important people and events.

Each culture has its own special days. Many of our holidays came to us from Europe. One is Valentine's Day. Europeans have celebrated this day for hundreds of years. The Irish brought us St. Patrick's Day.

Some days are important in more than one culture. For Japanese Americans, the fifth of May is Children's Day. For Mexican Americans, the same day is Cinco de Mayo (SINK-oh day MY-oh). This holiday honors a famous battle in Mexican history.

December is a month full of holidays. Kwanzaa honors the culture of African Americans and lasts for a week. Jewish people celebrate the eight days of Hanukkah. People in many Christian cultures share the holiday of Christmas.

We celebrate the new year in different ways, too. For many of us, New Year's Day is the first day of January. For many Chinese people, the new year starts on a different date each year. The Chinese New Year celebration goes on for 15 days.

What holidays do people celebrate where you live? Which ones do you share with your family and friends?

Many people like to light candles for Kwanzaa, a holiday that honors African American culture.

5. Our Community Shares Different Traditions

You can see people take part in activities that happen every year. These activities are traditions. What traditions do Americans share?

Every culture has its own traditions. Games and sports are part of these traditions. So are arts, such as music and dance. Other traditions can involve wearing certain clothes or doing other special things.

Many of our sports began as traditions in certain cultures. Do you like to play soccer? This sport came to us from Europe. So did golf, skiing, and ice-skating. Surfing came from the culture of the Hawaiian Islands.

Our game of soccer comes from England.

We also enjoy gifts from many cultures in our music and other arts. Jazz, rock and roll, and types of gospel music all grew out of African American music. Salsa and tango come from Latino cultures. Japanese Americans share Kabuki, a kind of drama, or play.

Many cultures have their own dances. Do you know how to clog? Clogging was started in the United States by people from Ireland, Scotland, and other countries. How about the hula? This style of dancing comes to us from Hawaii.

What are some traditions that people share where you live? What are some favorite traditions in your family?

Some types of gospel music came from African American music.

6. Our Community Expresses Itself

People take pride in expressing their culture. Two ways that they do this is through writing and artwork. Many artists and writers show their cultural backgrounds in their work.

Kadir Nelson is an African American artist. His paintings are of African American culture. Some of his work shows famous African Americans. Others shows those who are struggling.

Tomie dePaola is a writer of Italian and Irish heritage. He wrote children books. His most famous book is *Strega Nona*. In the story, Strega Nona is an Italian woman who makes pasta. Strega is from the same place as dePaola's ancestors who came to America.

Kadir Nelson's paintings focus on African American culture.

Carmen Lomas Garza is a Mexican American artist. Garza painted the beauty in everyday Mexican American life. One of her paintings shows a birthday celebration with people dancing and talking. There is even a piñata. Celebrations are an important part of Mexican American culture.

Amy Tan is an Asian American writer. Tan is part of a Chinese immigrant family. Her most famous book, *The Joy Luck Club*, is about Chinese immigrants. The book follows four mothers and daughters in immigrant families. The story describes their experiences as immigrants in the United States.

These people create these works for different reasons. Sometimes they just want to express their backgrounds. Others find that their culture brings out their best work. And others do it to inform others and bring change.

Amy Tan wrote *The Joy Luck Club*. The characters in the book have the same cultural background as Tan.

Lesson Summary

Our communities are very diverse. People in our country have come from around the world. With them, they have brought cultures that influence American culture.

You can see how diverse American culture is by studying the community around you. You see it in the foods we eat and in the languages we speak. You can see it in our holidays and in our traditions. Does our diverse country make your life more interesting? What do you think?

 Geography History

Many People, Many Ways of Life

Our land has been home to diverse cultures for thousands of years. Once, many groups of American Indians lived here. Each group had its own way of life. What were these cultures like, and how did they differ from each other?

Hello! Welcome to the Time Travel Express! This is a very special train. It travels through time as well as space!

Today the train will take us into the past to meet three groups of American Indians. We will see how they lived before large numbers of new settlers came to their lands.

Our first stop is the year 1600, in what is now the state of New Jersey. There we will meet a group called the Lenapes (luh-NAHP-ees). All aboard!

Lenapes gather inside a longhouse.

The Lenapes

The Time Travel Express is taking us along the Delaware River. Later, this area will become part of the Northeast region of the United States. In 1600, it is home to the Lenape people.

We stop by a village near the river. Do you see the large houses with curved roofs?

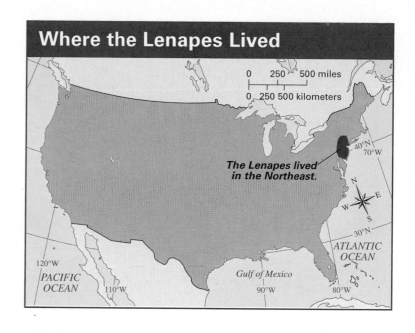

Where the Lenapes Lived

The Lenapes lived in the Northeast.

They are called longhouses. Several families can share one longhouse. The smaller round houses are called wigwams.

The Lenapes fish in the river. They get many of the other things they need in forests nearby. They use wood and bark from trees to build their houses. They also hunt deer and beavers. They use the skins from the animals to make clothes.

There are also gardens in the village for growing crops. There, the Lenape women grow food, such as corn, beans, and squash. Many American Indians in this region grow these three crops. The crops are known as "the three sisters."

The Lenapes lived in the Northeast.

Many Lenape families lived in small round houses called wigwams.

Where the Chumash Lived

0   250   500 miles
0   250   500 kilometers

40°N
70°W

The Chumash lived near the Pacific Ocean.

N
E
W
S

30°N

ATLANTIC OCEAN

120°W

PACIFIC OCEAN
110°W

Gulf of Mexico
90°W

80°W

The Chumash lived near the Pacific Ocean.

This mural shows Chumash traveling in a boat. The men used wood from trees to make their canoes.

The Chumash

Next, the Time Travel Express takes us to the Pacific Coast in the year 1750. One day, this place will be part of California. The city of Santa Barbara will grow up nearby.

We stop near a village that looks out on the Pacific Ocean. The village was built by the Chumash (CHOO-mash). Many Chumash live along the Pacific Coast or on nearby islands.

About 500 people live in this village. The village has many dome-shaped houses. The Chumash cut branches from willow trees to make frames for their houses. Then they cover the frames with mats made from reeds, a type of plant.

Look out to sea. The men are out there in long, narrow boats called canoes. They are using long, sharp spears to hunt for seals, tuna, and whales.

On land, the men hunt deer and other animals, while the women also help to gather food. They look for berries, wild plants, and acorns. The Chumash eat acorn soup or acorn cakes every day.

The Chumash made these colorful cave paintings.

In Chumash groups, women can become leaders. A woman is the chief of this village. The chief tries to keep everyone safe and tries to make sure that no one goes hungry.

The Chumash wear little clothing because the climate in this region is so mild. Sometimes the men wear just a belt to carry tools. The women wear skirts made of deerskin or woven from plants.

As we leave the village, watch for a cave nearby. Inside, colorful pictures cover the walls and ceilings. Religious leaders probably draw these pictures. It is their way of asking the gods to help the Chumash live a good life.

Where the Comanches Lived

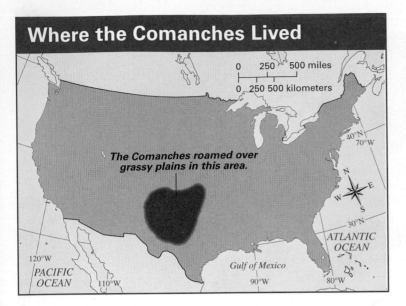

The Comanches roamed over grassy plains in this area.

The Comanches roamed the grassy plains in Texas.

Our last stop is in the year 1775. We are hundreds of miles to the east of the Pacific Ocean. Grassy plains stretch as far as we can see. One day, this place will be part of Texas. Right now, it is home to many groups of Comanches (kuh-MAN-cheez).

Over there, some women are setting up tepees. Tepees are a kind of tent. They are easy to set up and take down. This is important to the Comanches because they are always moving from one place to another.

Why are the Comanches always moving? They move because they must follow bison herds. The Comanches have built their way of life around the bison. Bison meat gives them food, and the women make clothes and blankets from the skins. Even the tepees are made from bison skins.

Comanche's lived in tepees because they were constantly on the move. Comanche women could put up a tepee in about 15 minutes.

The Comanches get other useful things from the bison, too. They make tools such as sewing needles from bison bones. They use the horns to make bowls and cups. They even use the bison stomach as a strong water bag.

The men and boys hunt the bison with bows and arrows. They make most of the bows out of wood, but sometimes they make bows from bison horns.

The Comanches used to hunt on foot. But then people from Europe brought horses to North America. The Comanches quickly became very skilled horseback riders. With horses, they can travel much farther to hunt bison. They also ride horses in battles against their enemies.

Our train is rolling again. We are returning to our starting place in our own time. I hope you have enjoyed our trip into the past! ◆

Comanches were skilled hunters of bison on the grassy plains.

Making Communities Better

How do people improve their communities?

Introduction

Our communities bring us many good things. They are full of diverse people and interesting places. But communities have problems, too. When people see these problems, they can help solve them. Every person has a chance to improve their community. Just one person can make a big difference.

In this lesson, you will learn why helping improve your community is an important part of being a good citizen. You will also learn how improving your community benefits everyone who lives in it.

You will also read about five people who set out to solve problems in their own communities. Other people did not always like what these five people did at first. But in the end, these people each made their town or city a better place to live. Their work also helped people in many other places. What problems do you see in your community?

Social Studies Vocabulary

boycott
canal
citizenship
common good
disabled
strike

◄ These kids are cleaning up their local park. By cleaning up the park, they are improving their community.

 Civics Economics Geography History

To be a good citizen, you should treat your classmates with respect.

citizenship the rights and responsibilities of citizens

1. Good Citizens Help Their Community

You are part of a community in the United States. And it is important that you help out your community. This is part of good **citizenship**. All people in our country should practice good citizenship.

There are many things you can do every day to be a good citizen. You should treat everyone around you with respect. No matter how they look or act, all your classmates are equals. You must treat them this way at all times.

The United States has laws that you have to follow. These laws tell you that you cannot steal or try to hurt other people. If you see someone breaking a law, it is your job either to stop them or to tell someone else.

As you grow older, you will gain more responsibilities. One day, you may have a family to support. For this reason, you should work hard in school. When you get a job, you should do your best at it. One day, you will also be allowed to vote. Voting is another way to contribute to the community.

You should do your part in keeping the **common good**. The common good is what is best for everyone in your community. Keeping your community clean is one example of contributing to the common good. When someone litters, everyone is affected.

These are some of the things that all people of the United States have a responsibility to do. But some people go above and beyond these duties to make their community a better place. You will read about five people who practiced excellent citizenship.

common good the things that are good for everyone in a community

Volunteering is one way to practice good citizenship. These people are helping their community by building a house.

Clara Barton helped many different people during her life.

2. Clara Barton Helps Soldiers

From early in her life, Clara Barton wanted to help others. When her brother suffered a severe injury after falling from a roof, she cared for him. In 1838, when she was a teenager, Barton began teaching at a Massachusetts schoolhouse.

Most teachers at this time were men, but Barton was very good at teaching. She opened a free school so that kids who could not afford other schools could get an education. Within just a year, the school had grown to 600 students under Barton's direction. But because she was a woman, the school board did not hire her as the head of the school.

This did not slow Barton's desire to help people. When the Civil War began, Barton was able to help. Her father had been part of the military and had encouraged her to care for soldiers during the war.

At first, she gathered medical supplies and treated soldiers returning from the battlefield. But where she really wanted to be was the front lines. Very few women went near the battlefields, but this did not stop Barton.

When she got there, she did whatever she could to help out. She cleaned hospitals, cared for soldiers, and even risked her life coming to the aid of wounded soldiers. Soldiers called her the "Angel of the Battlefield."

After the war, Barton continued her service to the communities around her. She founded the American Red Cross, which helped people after disasters like floods or fires. She was the organization's first president. You may have heard of the Red Cross. That's because the American Red Cross still helps people all over the country.

Thanks to Barton, people can get help from the American Red Cross after a natural disaster. The people here are getting supplies after an earthquake.

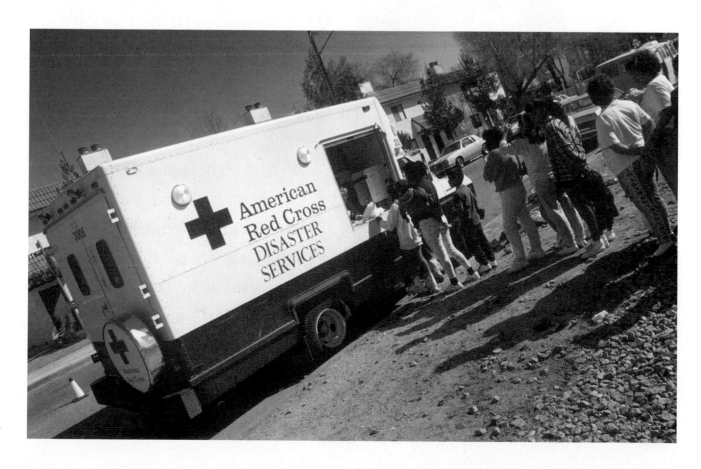

strike when workers stop working to try to get something they want, such as better pay

3. César Chávez Helps Farmworkers

César (SAY-zahr) Chávez was born near Yuma, Arizona, and came from a poor family. When he was still young, César and his family moved to California. As a teenager, he became a migrant farmworker to help his family.

Migrant farmworkers often had hard lives. They worked long hours for very little pay. Often workers got sick or hurt because they had to use unsafe chemicals and machines. César and his family also faced many hardships as farmworkers.

As a young man, César wanted to help the farmworkers. In 1962, he helped to start a new group, which became known as the United Farm Workers of America, or UFW. The UFW helped farmworkers ask for better pay and safer working conditions.

At that time, César lived in the town of Delano, California. There were farms all around the town. At first, the farm owners there refused to listen to the UFW. So César told all the workers to stop picking the crops. Stopping work in this way is called a **strike**. César hoped the strike would make the owners pay more attention to the workers.

César Chávez made life better for farmworkers.

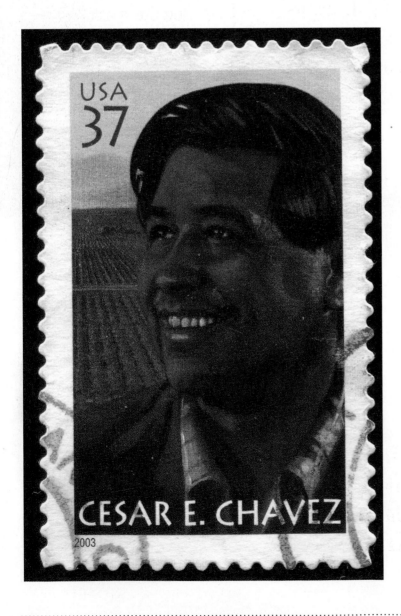

The owners still didn't listen. César took another step. He asked people to stop buying what the farms sold. This is called a **boycott**.

It took César and the UFW five years, but many of the farm owners finally gave in. They agreed to pay the farmworkers more and also promised to make the work safer.

César Chávez helped to make Delano a better place for farmworkers. He went on to help farmworkers in many other places around the country for the next thirty years. César helped them get better pay and safer ways of working.

These people are marching to show their support for the UFW.

boycott when people refuse to buy products from a certain business

4. Ruby Bridges Helps African Americans

In 1960, Ruby Bridges was six years old and ready to start first grade. When she did, she would make history.

Ruby lived in New Orleans, Louisiana. At that time, black students and white students in New Orleans went to different schools. Ruby would be the first African American to go to the white school near her home.

Many white people were upset. They wanted black and white students to be kept apart. Still, Ruby's mother was hopeful. She thought the school was a good one. And she thought that it was time that black and white children went to the same schools. But Ruby's father was worried. "We're just asking for trouble," he said.

Ruby's first day of school was frightening. Outside the school, crowds of angry people threw things at her and yelled that blacks didn't belong in their schools. Ruby thought some of them might even hurt her.

Ruby Bridges made history when she was just six years old.

Inside the school, Ruby discovered that she was the only student in her classroom. All the others had stayed home.

For months, Ruby was the only student in her class. Still, she kept coming to school. People started to see that she wasn't going away. When she returned to school the next year, many students had returned to their classes.

Ruby made it easier for all children in New Orleans to go to good schools together. As an adult, Ruby helps people in other communities, too. She talks to children and adults about her experience and how we can still learn from it today.

Ruby helped to show people that black and white children could go to the same schools.

5. Lois Marie Gibbs Helps Make Her Community Safer

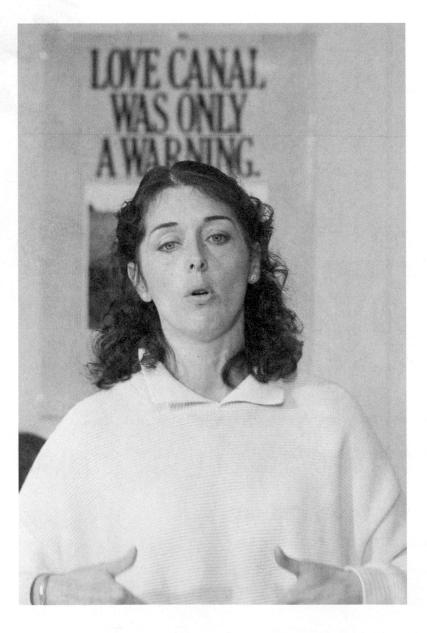

canal a waterway made by humans

Lois Gibbs wanted to know why children near Love Canal were getting sick.

In 1978, Lois Marie Gibbs lived in Niagara Falls, New York. Lois had two children, Michael and Melissa. Michael became very sick. Lois wanted to know why.

There was an old **canal,** or waterway, near Michael's school called Love Canal. Businesses had been dumping dangerous chemicals into the canal for years before it was buried.

The school playground was built were the canal used to be. Lois thought the old canal was making her children sick. Lois didn't know what to do. No one believed her fears about Love Canal.

Lois asked her neighbors about their health. It turned out that many of the children in the area were sick. Some scientists agreed that the canal could be the problem.

Lois decided to do something about it. She got all her neighbors together. Lois and her neighbors knew they needed help. They decided to tell everyone they could about their problem.

Lois and her neighbors made signs to carry. Then they followed the governor of New York around. People saw them on television.

Finally, the governor came to visit Love Canal. He agreed to help families move to a safer place. Later, President Jimmy Carter helped, too.

Lois Gibbs made a big difference in her community. Later, she helped people in other towns and cities. She showed them how to join together to make their communities safer places to live in.

This school was closed because of the chemicals in Love Canal.

disabled not being able to do an everyday thing, such as walk, in the same way that most people can

Judy Heumann started the group Disabled in Action.

6. Judy Heumann Helps Disabled People

Judy Heumann (HEW-man) was born in 1947. When she was a baby, she got sick with polio. This disease hurt her legs. Judy would never be able to walk. She had to use a wheelchair to get around.

Judy lived in Brooklyn, New York. On her first day of first grade, her mother brought her to school. The principal wouldn't let Judy in because she was in a wheelchair. A teacher came to Judy's house for a few hours each week instead.

When Judy was in fourth grade, she was finally allowed to go to school. There she met other **disabled** students. Disabled means not being able to do an everyday thing, like walk, talk, hear, or learn, in the same way that most people can. Judy learned that the other disabled students felt the same way she did. Her legs didn't work right, but she wanted to learn as much as any other student.

In college, Judy studied to be a teacher. At first, New York City wouldn't let her teach because she was in a wheelchair. Judy went to court to win the right to teach.

Thanks to Judy, disabled students are treated more fairly.

In 1970, Judy formed a group called Disabled in Action. She started the group to protect disabled people in New York from being treated unfairly. The group has grown a lot since then. It helps disabled people all across the country to live better lives.

After creating Disabled in Action, Judy worked closely with the government of the United States. She helped to make sure that people who are disabled have the same rights as everyone else under the law. She continues to fight for the rights of disabled people today.

Lesson Summary

In this lesson, you learned ways to practice good citizenship. You also met five people who showed how to be good citizens. Clara Barton, César Chávez, Ruby Bridges, Lois Marie Gibbs, and Judy Heumann all helped to improve their communities. They made the lives of the people around them better. Their work helped people in many other places, too.

You, too, can make a difference in your community. There are things that you can do every day to lend a hand. What can you think of doing to make your community a better place?

Civics    Geography

Helping a Community in Need

Sometimes problems are too big for a town or a city to solve by itself. In 2005, a storm put most of New Orleans under water. Homes and businesses were ruined. Thousands of people had no food or shelter. Who reached out to help? How did the city recover?

In 2005, a big storm hit New Orleans, a city in Louisiana. The storm flooded many parts of the city.

The city of New Orleans sits on very low ground near two large lakes. Years ago, levees, or walls, were built to keep the lakes' water from flooding the city. However, in 2005, a huge storm struck New Orleans. Afterward, many of the levees that helped keep water out of the city broke.

Water poured into the streets of New Orleans. The storm wrecked homes, flooded streets, and trapped people and animals. People living in the city had to find new places to stay. New Orleans needed help—and lots of it.

New Orleans

Mississippi

Louisiana

Lake Ponchartrain

Mississippi River

New Orleans

30°N

0 25 50 miles
0 25 50 kilometers

Gulf of Mexico

90°W

This Salvation Army volunteer passes out food.

Helping People Survive

The storm that struck New Orleans was called Hurricane Katrina. Hurricanes are large storms with heavy rains and powerful winds. These storms can cause a lot of harm. So can other events in nature, such as earthquakes. When events like storms or earthquakes cause a lot of damage, they are called **natural disasters**.

In a natural disaster, people need help. Organizations like the Red Cross and the Salvation Army gave help. These organizations are nonprofits, which means that they do not make money. Many of their workers are **volunteers**. These nonprofits help people in need around the world.

Hurricane Katrina struck a large area in the southern United States. Much of New Orleans was flooded, but other places were hit hard, too. Workers from the Red Cross and the Salvation Army rushed to the scene. They set up shelters for people who had lost their homes throughout the area, brought drinking water and other supplies, and cooked hot meals. They helped many people survive the disaster.

This photograph of Hurricane Katrina was taken from space.

natural disaster an event in nature, such as an earthquake or flood, that causes great harm

volunteer a person who agrees to do a task without being paid for it

SPCA helped animals that were affected by Hurricane Katrina.

Saving Animals

People were not the only ones needing help in New Orleans. After Hurricane Katrina, pets were in trouble, too. A group called the SPCA reached out to help these pets.

SPCA stands for the Society for the Prevention of Cruelty to Animals. The SPCA has been helping animals in need for more than 100 years. Like the Red Cross, it is a nonprofit.

The day before Katrina struck, the SPCA took 263 pets to Houston, Texas. It wanted to keep them out of danger. But the real work started after the flood. Dogs, cats, horses, and other pets were stranded. Many of them died. Still, the SPCA rescued about 8,500 animals and worked to bring pets and their owners back together.

Kids Helping Out

Many kids lost almost all of their possessions because of the storm. Three girls from Maryland wanted to help these kids, so they started Project Backpack. They asked people to donate backpacks for kids affected by the storm. In two months, they collected about 50,000 backpacks! People from 25 states joined in to help them.

Girl Scout troops helped, too. They collected supplies for people who were hurt by Katrina. Different Girl Scout troops set up boxes in their schools and around their towns. The troops shipped supplies like food, candles, and blankets to people affected by the hurricane.

Have you ever heard the saying "Every little bit helps"? That was very true after Katrina. Large groups reached out to help, and so did many individuals. You can be sure that each little bit of help made a big difference.

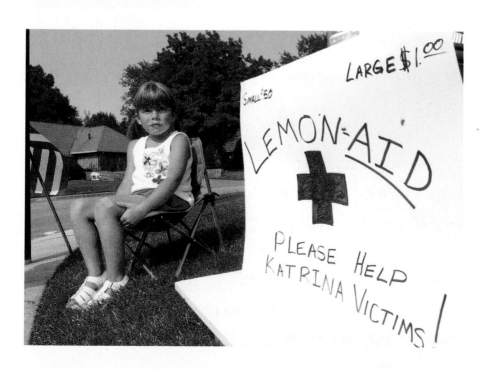

This girl is selling lemonade to raise money for people who were harmed by Hurricane Katrina.

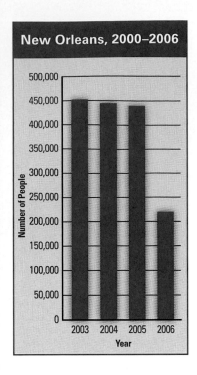

New Orleans, 2000–2006

As shown on this graph, many people left New Orleans after Katrina struck in 2005.

Finding New Homes

Hurricane Katrina flooded homes in New Orleans. At the time, about 500,000 people lived there. They had to find new places to stay, at least for a while.

Many people went to the Superdome, New Orleans's football stadium. Beds, food, and water were set up for those who needed them. But there wasn't enough room for everyone.

Houston, Texas, opened its arms to those who needed shelter. Many people stayed at a football stadium there, the Astrodome. Some went to other cities in Louisiana, while others moved to states like Georgia and Mississippi.

After the damage from the hurricane was cleared, some returned to New Orleans. But many stayed in the cities they moved to. A year after the storm, only about 200,000 people lived in New Orleans.

After Katrina, many people moved from New Orleans to cities nearby. This map shows some of the cities they moved to.

Where People Moved After Katrina

Rebuilding the City

After Hurricane Katrina, New Orleans was emptier. There were fewer businesses and people. Still, many stayed to rebuild their city.

People in each community worked together to rebuild their part of the city. They faced challenges. Rebuilding the city was hard and costly. But slowly, businesses started reopening. Neighborhoods also slowly recovered.

Many of those who left New Orleans missed the city. Over time, more people moved back.

Katrina affected New Orleans greatly, but after many years, it is on its way to recovery. People gather in New Orleans for celebrations like Mardi Gras and to cheer for sport teams. Tourists visit to experience New Orleans's music, food, and culture. There is still much to celebrate about the city. ◆

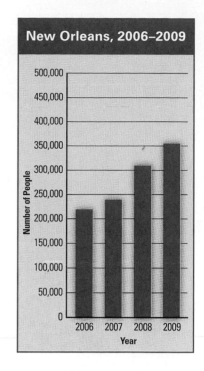

People moved back to New Orleans over the years.

People gather in Jackson Square in New Orleans for the Superbowl.

Cultures Around the World

How are people around the world alike and different?

Introduction

You and your friends probably do many of the same things every day. But your life may have been very different if you had been born in another country. What do you think children in other parts of the world do?

Some things are the same no matter where we live. Everyone eats and sleeps. Nearly all children play. In most places, children also go to school. But they don't all do these things in exactly the same way. In fact, in some places, children's lives are very different from yours.

In this lesson, you will read about the lives of children in six different countries. As you read, think about how each child's day is like yours and how it is different.

◄ Children from different places may have different ways of life. But many children around the world go to school every day just like you.

Geography

London has things that are similar to and different from American cities. One difference is that cars in London drive on the left side of the road instead of the right side.

1. Cultures in Different Countries

You are very familiar with the way you and your family live. But how do people in other parts of the world live? Do you think their lives are similar to or different from yours?

Different cultures affect how people live. Culture is made of different things. Food, clothes, and everyday activities are all parts of culture. However, what people eat, wear, and do each day change from place to place.

Some countries have cultures that are very similar to America's, while others have cultures that are different. If you visit a city in Canada, it might not look any different than a city in the United States. If you went to a city in India, however, it might look very different.

The **environment** can influence a country's culture. For example, rice is a common food in many countries in Asia. This is because the wet climate there is ideal for growing rice.

The environment can also affect the clothes people wear. In warm places like countries in central Africa, people tend to wear lighter clothing. In colder places like northern Russia, they need thick clothes to stay warm.

The environment also affects where people live. For example, the country of Japan is an island with many mountains inland. It is hard to build homes on the mountains, so few people live inland. Instead, most of the people live in cities along the coast, where land is flatter. Also, the ocean provides food and transportation for the people living near it.

As you read, think about how the environment has affected culture in each country. How does it compare to culture in America?

environment
Earth's air, water, soil, and living things

Many parts of Asia have a wet climate, which is ideal for growing rice. This is why rice is such an important part of the culture in these countries.

Josie's family goes ice fishing on the weekends.

Josie lives in the northern part of Canada.

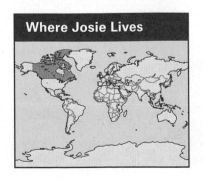

Where Josie Lives

2. Josie Lives in Canada

Josie lives in a small town in northern Canada. Josie's family is Inuit (IH-noo-wet). The Inuit people have lived in Canada for 3,000 years or more.

It is cold and snowy most of the year where Josie lives. Josie skis to school. Her best friend, Ivy, rides to school on a snowmobile. At school, they eat a hot breakfast.

Josie is learning to use a computer at school. Her other classes are reading, math, and history. Josie doesn't speak English. She speaks Inuktitut (ih-NOOK-teh-toot) with her family and friends.

On weekends, Josie's family sometimes goes ice fishing. They make holes in the ice and try to catch fish in the water below. Josie also likes to play in the snow with her dog, Max.

One of Josie's favorite meals is caribou stew. Caribou are large deer that live in Josie's part of the world.

Josie's warmest boots are handmade from sealskin. Some of her blankets are made of sealskin, too. Josie, Ivy, and their friends use the blankets to play a blanket toss game. Lots of people play together. Several people hold the edges of the sealskin blanket. One person stands in the middle of the blanket, and the others toss him or her into the air. Josie and Ivy both love to bounce on the blanket.

Josie and her friends like to play blanket toss.

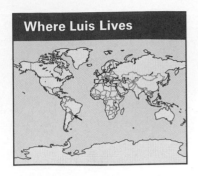

Luis lives on a farm in Paraguay.

Luis's father works hard in the fields.

3. Luis Lives in Paraguay

Luis lives on a farm in a country in South America called Paraguay. He lives with his mother, father, and three brothers.

Luis wakes up before sunrise every morning so he can help his father and brothers in the fields. There's always something to be done on the farm. Luis might plant seeds, hoe weeds, or pick crops.

Luis and his family often take a break to drink terere (teh-reh-REH). Terere is made in a cup with water and dried, crushed leaves. The cup is called a guampa (WAHM-pah). The guampa is usually made from a cow's horn. Luis sips the drink through a metal straw. The straw has a strainer at one end to keep the leaves out.

Luis and his brother ride their horse to school five days a week.

Luis goes to school five days a week. He and his brother Esteban (es-TAY-bahn) ride their family's horse to school, which is several miles from their farm.

Luis's favorite part of school is playing with his friends. During breaks, they play soccer. They call the game fútbol (FOOT-bohl).

Most of Luis's classes are in Spanish. However, outside of class, Luis and his friends like to speak Guarani (gwahr-uh-NEE). Guarani is a language that people in Paraguay have spoken for hundreds of years. Luis likes the fact that people still speak Guarani today.

The bedrooms in Kazuo's house have shoji and futons.

Kazuo lives by the coast in Japan.

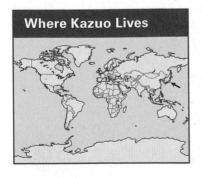

Where Kazuo Lives

4. Kazuo Lives in Japan

Kazuo (KAH-zoo-oh) lives in Tokyo (TOH-kee-OH). Tokyo is a large city by the ocean in the country of Japan.

Each morning, Kazuo wakes up in the room he shares with his little brother. The rooms in Kazuo's house are small because many people live in Tokyo, and housing there is expensive.

Kazuo's room has sliding doors made of paper. These doors are called shoji (shoh-gee). Kazuo and the rest of his family sleep on thick mattresses called futons. Each morning, they roll up their futons and blankets and put them in the closet.

For breakfast, Kazuo and his brother eat cereal. His parents eat rice and egg with chopsticks.

After breakfast, Kazuo's father hurries to catch the train to work. Kazuo's mother stays home to take care of his little brother.

Meanwhile, Kazuo gets ready for school. After he gets his schoolbag, he goes to the front door to put on his shoes. Kazuo's family members never wear shoes in the house.

Kazuo goes to school six days a week. He rides the bus with his friends. They all wear navy blue uniforms. Kazuo speaks Japanese with his friends, but in school he is studying English.

Kazuo and his friends practice a sport called kendo (ken-doh) in gym class. In kendo, the boys use bamboo sticks like swords. They put on face masks and gloves so they don't get hurt.

Kazuo and his friends practice kendo for fun.

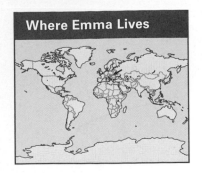

Where Emma Lives

Emma lives in a small city in Hungary.

Emma feeds her geese every morning before school.

5. Emma Lives in Hungary

Emma lives in a small city in Hungary, a country in central Europe. Emma lives in an old house with her mother and two brothers.

Every morning, Emma feeds the geese in the backyard. Then she eats breakfast before walking to school with her brothers, Viktor and Sandor (SHAN-dor).

Emma is in third grade. Her favorite class is music. All students in Hungary must learn a foreign language. Emma is learning French. However, she speaks Hungarian with her friends.

Emma and her brothers are good at sports. Viktor plays soccer. Sandor is on the school's swim team. Their school has an indoor swimming pool. Emma practices gymnastics in school twice a week. Her favorite thing to do in gymnastics is the parallel bars.

Emma has music lessons on Tuesday afternoons. She is learning to play the flute. Her mother thinks Emma plays beautiful music. But her brothers cover their ears when she plays. Someday, Emma wants to play the flute in an orchestra like her uncle Zoltan (ZOHL-tahn).

Emma likes to show her skill on the parallel bars.

Paul and his family raise cattle on their ranch.

Paul lives on a ranch in Australia.

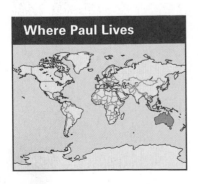

6. Paul Lives in Australia

Paul lives on a cattle ranch in the country of Australia. The cattle ranch is far from any city or town. Australians call this part of their country the outback. It's hot and dusty in the outback.

When Paul gets up in the morning, he puts on a T-shirt and jeans. Then he puts on tall leather boots. He wears a hat to keep the sun off his neck.

Paul eats eggs and snags, or sausages, for breakfast. After breakfast, Paul takes care of his horse, Scout. Later in the day, he'll ride out with his father to check on the cattle.

Paul and his two sisters go to school for an hour and a half a day. Actually, they don't go to school—school comes to them!

The school is called Schools of the Air. It allows them to go to school through their computer. The teacher and students can see each other using cameras on their computer. Paul spends his school day listening to the teacher and doing lessons. Then he does his homework.

Paul would rather be eating a sandwich than doing homework. Paul spreads a brown paste made from vegetables on bread or crackers. It's his favorite snack.

Once a week, Paul's family drives to the store in town. Sometimes they stop at another ranch to see if their friends need anything. Paul's friend, Gary, lives on this ranch. Paul and Gary like to play video games and ride their horses.

Paul goes to school through a computer.

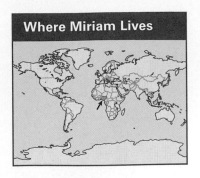

Miriam lives in a town in Nigeria.

Miriam works hard in school.

7. Miriam Lives in Nigeria

Miriam lives in a town in Nigeria, a country in Africa. Miriam has 11 brothers and sisters. She helps look after the younger ones. She likes to use her doll to play-act stories for them.

Miriam likes school. She does well in math and geography. She also studies history and health.

Everyone speaks English at school. Miriam also speaks Hausa (HOW-seh). Hausa is one of hundreds of languages in Nigeria.

After school, Miriam watches television. Then she does her homework.

After homework, it's time for dinner. Food in Nigeria can be very spicy. People often cook with hot peppers. Miriam eats a lot of rice, beans, corn, and yams. She also eats fruit every day. Mangoes are her favorite.

Miriam also likes a soft drink that is made with ginger. Ginger is the spice used in gingerbread. Miriam likes the taste of ginger.

Miriam is learning to play the drums. "Talking drums" are an important part of juju music. Juju songs tell stories about local people and events. People play juju songs in the evenings. Miriam dances to the music with her friends.

Drums are an important part of Nigeria's culture.

Lesson Summary

You have just read about children in six places around the world. In many ways, their lives are alike. For example, all of them go to school.

But in other ways, their lives are very different. They eat different foods and do different things to have fun. These differences come from the cultures in each country. What about you? How is your life like those of the children you read about? How is it different?

 Geography History

The Story of Mexico City

One reason that people around the world are different is that each place has its own past. How does the history of Mexico City help us to understand the people who live there today?

Carlos lives in Mexico City, the biggest city in Mexico. It is also Mexico's capital. A capital is the city where the government of a country meets.

Carlos's sister, Myra, has been learning about the city's past in school. Today she is taking Carlos on a tour to share what she has learned.

This is the main square in Mexico City.

"We'll start at the main square," Myra says. "That's where the story of our city begins."

This serpent head sculpture was part of an Aztec temple.

The Aztecs

At the square, Myra tells Carlos how Mexico City grew.

"It all starts with the Aztecs," Myra says. "The first city on this spot was built by the Aztecs. The Aztecs were an American Indian group. They built a great capital city here in 1325 and called it Tenochtitlán (tay-noch-teet-LAHN). You can still see parts of Aztec buildings around the square today.

"The Aztecs told an interesting story about why they built their city here," Myra goes on. "The story says the Aztecs were looking for a place to settle. One of their gods told them to watch for an eagle sitting on a cactus. The eagle would be eating a snake."

"And the Aztecs found the eagle here?" Carlos asks.

That's right," Myra says. "But in those days, this was just a muddy island in the middle of a lake."

Mexico City is in the center of Mexico.

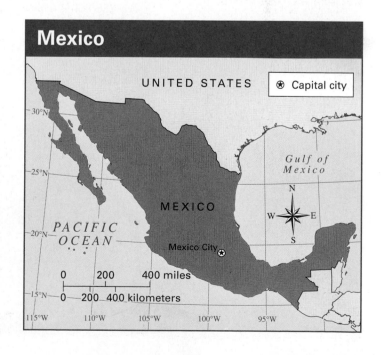

An Island City

"How could the Aztecs build a big city on an island in a lake?" Carlos asks.

"Well, they had to change their surroundings," Myra explains. "For instance, they built canals for boats so they could move around, and they built raised roads that crossed the lake. They even made new islands that they used as floating gardens. They grew flowers, beans, and other crops on the islands. Beans are still a big part of Mexican cooking today."

"Tenochtitlán sounds neat," Carlos says. "I wish I could have seen it."

"We can go see a famous painting of what it might have looked like," Myra tells him. "It's in the National Palace, right here on the square."

Diego Rivera, a Mexican artist, painted this picture of Tenochtitlán.

The End of Tenochtitlán

"So what happened to Tenochtitlán?" asks Carlos.

"The Aztecs were very powerful," Myra answers. "And their city was large and beautiful. But in the 1500s, the Spanish came to Mexico looking for gold. They joined together with some American Indians who were the Aztecs' enemies. They fought the Aztecs and won, and that was the end of Tenochtitlán."

"Why?" asks Carlos.

"Because the Spanish tore down the Aztecs' great city," Myra says. "Then they built their own city in its place. They called it Mexico City. 'Mexico' comes from another name for the Aztecs."

Myra points to a large church. "The Spanish built that church long ago on the spot where an Aztec temple once stood. The Spanish used stones from Aztec temples in many of their buildings. You can see still see old Aztec stones in some of these buildings today."

The Spanish built this church on the ruins of an Aztec temple.

A Mix of Cultures

"Spain ruled our country for 300 years," Myra goes on. "During this time, children of the Spanish and the Aztecs married. Their cultures mixed together. Meanwhile, the Spanish drained the lake around Mexico City. This let them build an even bigger city."

"But we aren't ruled by Spain any more," Carlos points out.

"That's right," Myra says. "In the 1800s, the people of Mexico rose up against Spain. After much fighting, they took control of their country. We still celebrate this event. A special bell hangs in the National Palace. The bell is rung once a year on September 15, the day before our Independence Day."

Carlos smiles. "So now the people were Mexicans like us."

Myra smiles too. "Yes, but the old cultures lived on. For instance, the people made buildings that mixed Spanish and Aztec styles. And we still speak Spanish today."

The National Palace is one of the old Spanish buildings in Mexico City.

Mexico City Today

"You see, Carlos," Myra says, "we are like these buildings. Most people in Mexico City come from both the American Indians and the Spanish. We have American Indian history in us, just like some of these buildings have Aztec stones."

"Mexico City has lots of brand-new buildings, too," Carlos says proudly.

"Oh, yes," Myra agrees. "Just look at the skyscrapers! Our city grew very fast in the 1900s. People came here to get jobs in factories and other businesses. Now our city is one of the biggest in the world."

"Hey, look!" Carlos points at a huge Mexican flag on a pole in the square. The flag shows an eagle standing on a cactus with a snake hanging from the eagle's beak.

"It's the old Aztec story!" Carlos says.

"That's right, Carlos," Myra answers. "The Aztecs are still with us, even in our flag." ◆

Today Mexico City is one of the biggest cities in the world.

The eagle in the middle of the Mexican flag represents an old Aztec story.

Understanding Our Economy

How do we buy and sell things?

Introduction

Have you ever been to a farmers' market? Farmers' markets are places where farmers sell the crops that they grow. People go to these markets so that they can buy different fruits and vegetables that they want.

Sometimes, people buy things from a farmers' market that they can take home, like fruits or vegetables. Other times people can pay for someone else to do something for them, like paint their faces.

But people cannot buy all of the things that they want. They have to choose between the different things that they want to buy.

How do buyers decide what to buy at a farmers' market? How do sellers try to get people to buy their produce? In this lesson, you'll explore the answers to these questions.

Social Studies Vocabulary

economy

free market economy

goods

market

scarcity

services

◀ People can buy many different things at a market. This man is buying different vegetables from this seller at a farmers' market.

$ Economics

Sellers want to sell the food they grow to buyers.

> **market** a place where buyers and sellers come together

1. We Buy and Sell Things

Suppose that you are at a farmers' market with your family. It is early summer. Many farmers have fruits to sell.

Farmers sell different foods that they grow in order to make money. A farmer is a seller at the **market**. A market is any place where buyers and sellers come together to trade.

In a farmers' market, you may notice that there are many different stands selling similar fruits and vegetables. These sellers want buyers to buy from their stand instead of someone else's. In a market, sellers must compete with one another to sell their goods and services to buyers. One way to compete is for sellers to lower the prices of the goods they sell.

Suppose that you are walking around a farmers' market with your family. You may stop and buy different fruits from the stands in the market to take home. When you do this, you are a buyer.

When you choose what fruit to buy, you want to get the best fruit that you can for the lowest price. You may check if the fruit is ripe and not bruised. You may shop around and look at different stands before you decide which fruit you want to buy.

Whenever you buy or sell something, you are part of our **economy**. An economy is made up of all the businesses in a place. Sometimes an economy can be small. The town that the farmers' market is in has an economy. All the businesses in the United States also make up an economy.

economy the system in which goods and services are bought and sold

Buyers can shop around for things to buy.

2. We Buy Goods and Services

At the farmers' market, people choose to spend their money on many different things. Some choose to spend their money on fruits. Other people may buy popcorn. Some can even pay to get their faces painted.

In an economy, people can choose to spend money on things called **goods** or **services**. Many businesses sell goods. Goods are items that you can use. There are many different goods that people can buy. Food, clothing, books, and even a house are examples of goods that people spend money on. Often, a good is something you can touch or see.

When people buy goods, they may use them just once or use them over and over again. The food you buy at the farmers' market is a good that you can only use once. If you buy a toy, you are buying a good that can be used many times.

goods items that can be bought, sold, and traded, such as food and computers

services tasks you pay someone to do for you

This stuffed animal is a good people can buy.

Some businesses sell services. A service is a task that someone does for you. Some people are paid to cut your hair or even teach you about new things. Unlike goods, you do not keep services that you buy.

People can provide services, like face painting, at farmers' markets. Some farmers' markets even have petting zoos. There are many animals that you can pet, like goats and sheep. You could pay a farmer to let you pet and feed the animals. You do not get to take or keep the animals you pet and feed.

The person who brought the animals to the farmers' market has provided a service by bringing the animals and letting you see and pet them. In our economy, people provide many different services for us. Think about services that you and your family use. What are some goods and services that you spend money on?

Going to a petting zoo is a service that you can buy.

3. The Things We Buy Are Scarce

When you look around the farmers' market for things to buy, look at how many goods each stand has. One stall may only have a small pile of apples left. Another person may only have one jar of honey left to sell. Your family may not be able to buy all the apples or honey that they want to.

People want many things. But our wants are always greater than the resources available to produce them. This is called **scarcity**.

Goods and services are scarce. At the farmers' market, each stand can sell different fruits and vegetables. But the farmers who grow the fruit only can make a certain amount each season. Since they can never grow enough fruits and vegetables for everyone to get as much as they want, these goods are scarce.

scarcity when people want more things than they can actually have

The amount of food that this girl can buy is limited.

Can your family spend as much time at the farmers' market as they want? There are only 24 hours in a day, and there are even less hours of sunlight. Time, like goods and services, is limited. Because of this, we can say that time is scarce.

If things are scarce, how can we get them? One way that we can get the things we want is by trading for them. But most people get what they want using money to purchase goods and services. We can buy something with money, and the seller can use this money to buy something else.

Do you have all the money that you want? The answer is probably "no." Because people don't have all the money they want, they must choose between the things they want to buy.

Once it gets dark, people cannot spend any more time at a farmers' market.

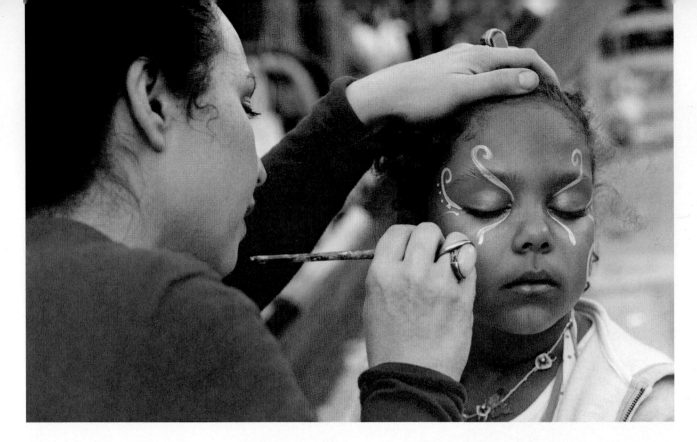

You should think about the costs and benefits of getting your face painted before you pay for it.

4. There Are Benefits and Costs to What We Buy

Buyers do not have enough money to buy everything that they want. They have to choose between the things that they want to have. To make this choice, people must think about the benefits and costs of the things they are choosing between. A good choice is one where the benefits are greater than the costs.

While you are at the farmers' market, you may want to get your face painted and buy a bag of oranges to take home. But both the face painting and oranges cost $4, and you only have $5 to spend. You can only choose to buy one of these things.

When you make a choice, you must look at the benefits and cost of each option you have. Each option has some benefits, or something you will gain by choosing it. Making a choice also has a cost. A cost is what you give up when you make a decision.

If you pay to get your face painted, there are costs and benefits. The benefit of getting your face painted is that it is fun to show to other people. The cost of the face painting is that it will only last a day before you have to wash it off, and then your face will not be painted anymore. You will also not be able to have fresh oranges with your breakfast.

There are also costs and benefits of buying the oranges. The benefit of oranges is that they are healthy for you, and you will not be hungry. The cost is that oranges are food, and once you eat them, they are gone. You also will not be able to show off your cool face painting!

Looking at the costs and benefits, you may decide that oranges are more important to you. In our economy, people get to make decisions about what they want to buy.

You may buy the bag of oranges after thinking about the benefits.

5. The Free Market Economy

A farmers' market is part of the much larger economy of the United States. The economy of the United States is a **free market economy**. In this type of economy, buyers and sellers make most of the choices.

In some economies, a person, business, or government tells people what to do. In a free market economy, every person is free to make their own choices about what to buy and sell.

Suppose there is a farmer who grows apples. One day, the farmer decides to grow pears instead. The farmer is free to choose to do this.

When the farmer brings these pears to a market, a buyer can choose which fruits or vegetables to buy. The buyer can choose to buy the pears from the farmer. Both the buyer and seller can make their own choices in a free market economy.

free market economy an economy where choices are left up to each buyer and seller

This farmer can choose what crops to grow because of the free market economy.

In a free market, people are free to choose what jobs they want. Suppose there is a young woman who works on a farm. She might help grow food for a farmer to sell at a farmers' market. She could choose to quit her job and study to become a doctor or a scientist. She could also choose to start her own farm and grow crops to sell.

In a free market economy, people can choose what they want to do for a job.

Because sellers can make choices in a free market economy, they can sell many different types of goods and services. Buyers then have more choices in what to buy.

Lesson Summary

You have read about the different parts of a market and that people can buy goods and services. You also learned that a market, like a farmers' market, is part of a larger economy.

In a market, buyers and sellers come together to get what they want. Buyers have to make choices about what they want to buy. How do you spend your money in a market? What are things that you need and want? How do you choose what to buy?

$ Economics Geography History

Making Mail Faster

Sometimes businesses don't sell goods. They might sell services, like cutting hair or delivering mail. Businesses want people to buy their services. How can businesses competing lead to better services?

Suppose that your grandmother's birthday is tomorrow. You live in New York City. She lives on the other side of the country, in San Francisco, California. Can you get a birthday gift sent to her in time? Yes, you can pay a delivery company to ship your gift overnight.

Delivery of packages and other mail is a service you can buy. Mail delivery has gotten faster over time. Why? A big reason is that businesses compete for customers. One way to get more customers is to lower prices. Another way is to offer better goods or services.

Delivering packages is a service that many people around the country use.

Fast Ships and Stagecoaches

Mail delivery used to be a lot slower than it is today. In the 1840s, mail could take up to six months to get from New York City to San Francisco. The mail was sent by ship. It had to go all the way around South America!

Six months was a long time to wait for mail. People wanted faster mail. Businesses began to compete to make their customers happy. Some businesses began to use faster ships. Then a man named John Butterfield tried something new. In 1858, his mail company started delivering mail across the country by land. The mail was carried on stagecoaches. The company said it could get mail from Missouri to California in just 24 days. But it often took months. People still wanted faster mail.

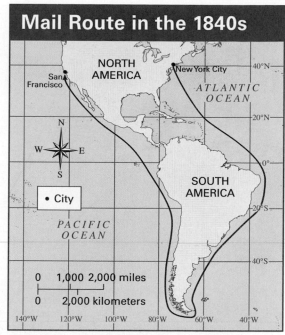

Mail Route in the 1840s

NORTH AMERICA

San Francisco

New York City

ATLANTIC OCEAN

40°N

20°N

0°

SOUTH AMERICA

20°S

• City

PACIFIC OCEAN

40°S

0   1,000 2,000 miles

0   2,000 kilometers

140°W   120°W   100°W   80°W   60°W   40°W

Ships had to sail all the way around South America to deliver mail.

A stagecoach would carry mail across the country.

Pony Express riders would change horses every few miles.

The Pony Express

In 1860, one man saw a chance to make money by creating an even faster mail service. His name was William H. Russell. He wouldn't use ships or stagecoaches. Instead, he would use fast horses and skilled riders to carry letters and other lightweight mail. Russell's new service became known as the Pony Express.

The Pony Express was designed for speed. A rider raced on horseback for about 10 to 15 miles. Then he changed horses and kept going. Each rider rode about 75 to 100 miles in a day. Then he tossed the mail he was carrying to a fresh rider. In this way, mail sped from Missouri to California in 10 days or less.

Competing with the Pony Express

Many people used the Pony Express to send their mail across the country. At around the same time, businesses began using new inventions to compete with the Pony Express to make sending mail faster.

Some businesses began sending mail over telegraph. The telegraph let people send messages to faraway places over electric wires. These messages were received almost at the same time that they were sent. But only words could be sent over the telegraph. People could not use the telegraph to send handwritten letters or packages around the country.

Other mail companies began to use trains to carry letters and packages. Large bags of mail could be carried anywhere that railroads could go. As more railroad tracks were laid down around the United States, the number of places that mail could be delivered grew. This made sending mail cheaper as well as faster. Because of competition from other businesses, the Pony Express lasted just 18 months.

Telegraphs could be used to send messages around the country.

Speedy trains picked up bags of mail without even stopping.

Airmail allowed people to send packages and letters overnight.

Mail Takes Flight

In the early 1900s, the invention of the airplane changed the way mail was sent around the country. Airplanes could move a lot faster than trains. They could carry mail across the country quicker and more easily than ever before.

In 1918, the first airmail was delivered by the U.S. Post Office Department. (Today, we call it the U.S. Postal Service.) But people also created new companies to ship mail this way.

In the 1970s, a man named Frederick W. Smith raised money to buy several airplanes. With his own airplanes, he made a bold claim. He created a company that promised to ship mail overnight. People loved the new service. Soon other companies offered overnight service, too.

Faster and Faster

Today, mail delivery continues to get quicker. With the Internet, people send e-mails to each other. People can also send letters, pictures, and videos to their friends and family instantly over the phone or on a tablet.

Other businesses are trying to make sending packages quicker and easier. Some businesses have been testing new technologies that can send you a package less than an hour after ordering it on the Internet. Soon, you may not need to wait even that long to get your letters and packages in the mail.

As you can see, mail delivery has become a lot faster over time. Why? It all starts with what people want. First, buyers must be willing to pay for something. Then, sellers will compete to find new ways to give buyers what they want. ◆

Today people can use the Internet to send mail.

Choices in a Free Market

Why do prices change in our economy?

Introduction

Think about the things you have at home. You might have clothes in a dresser. You might even have some toys to play with. You might have a computer that you can do homework and play games on, or you might have books that you can read. How do you get these things?

Your parents can buy you these things with money. Your parents or family members work so that they can earn money to buy what they want. You can also earn money to buy things that you want. In a free market economy, people can choose how they earn money.

People can choose what to buy with the money they earn. Sellers also choose what price to charge for the goods or services they provide.

How do sellers decide what prices to charge? Why do some things cost more than others? Why do prices for goods and services sometimes change? In this lesson, you will explore these questions.

> **Social Studies Vocabulary**
>
> demand
> incentive
> profit
> supply

◀ Your parents can buy you toys with the money they earn. They can choose how to earn money.

$ **Economics**

Teachers earn money by providing a service.

1. We Earn Money By Working

Suppose you are at a toy store. You may see a game that you really want to get for you and your friends to play. Like all goods, this game has a price tag that shows how much money you will need to buy it. How can you earn enough money to buy it?

In a free market economy, people are able to choose how to earn their money. Most people earn money by working. They may earn money by providing a service. For example, some people's parents are teachers. They can earn money by teaching students in the community.

At home, you might clean your room every week, help wash dishes, or maybe even take out the garbage. Your parents might pay you an allowance when you finish up all of your chores. If they do, they are paying you for a service.

People can also earn money by making something and selling it. Think about the things that are in the toy store. You might see action figures, stuffed animals, and toy cars. All of these things are made by people. People then sell these goods to you so that you can use them.

Think about the game that you want to buy. It could cost you $30. You might ask your parents to buy you the game. But your parents have to make money in order to buy things. How do your parents choose to make their money?

Maybe your parents own a business. In a business, people might make or sell goods, or they might help people by offering different services. Businesses pay people for the work that they do. In order to make money to pay people, a business needs to sell something. How do businesses choose what to sell?

This woman earns money by making toys to sell.

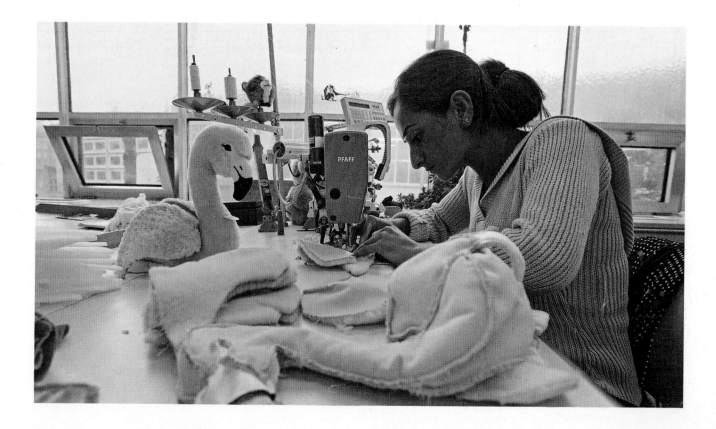

2. Businesses and the Economy

Think about the game you want to buy. The business that makes the game earns money when people buy it. But it also has to spend money in order to produce the game. The business buys different parts for the game and pays people to put it together.

In a free market economy, businesses want to earn a profit. **Profit** is the amount of money a business has left after it has paid for materials and workers. If a business sells their goods for more than it costs to make them, it will earn a profit.

Often, businesses make choices based on **incentives**. Incentives are things that lead businesses to make certain choices. More profit is one incentive. For example, a business might find a cheaper material to make a good with. Choosing cheaper materials will increase profits. This is an incentive to make more of this type of good.

profit the amount of money earned by a business after costs are removed

incentive something that leads a person to make a certain choice

A business might choose to use a cheaper fabric to make its goods.

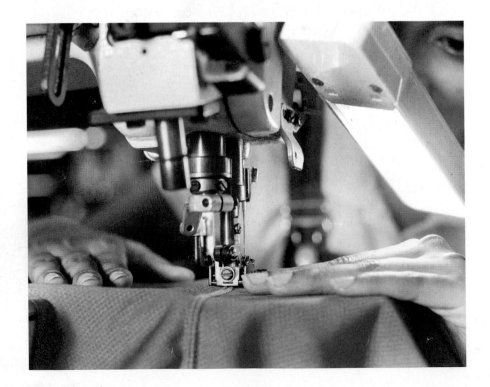

To make the most profit, you should choose the lemons that cost less money.

Rules or laws can force a business to spend more money on making its goods. The business might choose to raise prices for the goods it sells. Or it can choose to make something else instead.

If you want to start your own business to earn money, you must also think about profit. You want to sell something that will help you earn money for your game. You may choose to open a lemonade stand because lemonade is easy to make. Also, lemonade doesn't cost very much to make, so you can make a profit.

When you go to the grocery store to get your supplies, you may pick the lemons that cost the least money. Keeping costs low would help you make a profit for each glass of lemonade that you sell. Once you have made your lemonade, how much do you choose to sell each glass for?

Changes in laws can lead to higher gas prices.

When few people want a good, demand is low.

3. Prices Change When Supply Is High and Demand Is Low

In a free market economy, you can choose what price to sell your lemonade for. You could first choose to sell your lemonade for 50¢. If it only cost 5¢ to make each glass, you would make a profit of 45¢ per glass. However, would customers pay 50¢ for a cup of your lemonade?

In a free market, the price you choose to sell a good or service for is set by both the seller (you) and the buyer (the customers). This is also called **supply** and **demand**. Supply is the total amount of a good or service that is available to buy at any price. At your lemonade stand, the supply of lemonade is the amount of lemonade that you make to sell. Demand is the total amount of a good or service the customer in the market will buy at all prices.

Together, supply and demand set prices. Think about your new lemonade stand business. You might make five pitchers full of lemonade, so the supply of lemonade is high.

supply the total amount of a good or service available to buy

demand the total amount of a good or service that customers will buy at all prices

As you sit at your stand, you notice that not many people are buying lemonade from you. In fact, many people might already have lemonade to drink. They might be buying lemonade from a stand nearby, so they do not want to have more lemonade. This makes the demand for lemonade low.

You have a problem now. You have made more lemonade than customers want to buy. What do you think you can do?

One thing that you can do is lower the price of the lemonade. If you make the price of your lemonade low enough, customers might decide to buy some lemonade from you instead of the other stands. You can even make your prices lower than the other lemonade stands to compete with them. Lowering your prices could help you earn money. When supply is high and demand is low, prices go down.

If demand for your lemonade is low, you will need to lower the price of each glass.

4. Prices Change When Supply Is Low and Demand Is High

Sometimes many people want to buy the same thing, but there might not be enough of this good for everyone to buy one. Can you guess what happens to prices when supply is low and demand is high?

Suppose that you have been out at your lemonade stand for a few hours. The day has gotten very hot, and many people have been buying your lemonade. You might have already sold four full pitchers of lemonade, and now you only have one left.

When many people want a good, demand is high.

With only one pitcher of lemonade left, your supply of your lemonade is low. But in the hot weather, many customers still want to get lemonade. You might even have a long line of people waiting to buy lemonade from you. The demand for lemonade is high.

If demand for lemonade is high, you can raise the price of each glass.

Now the customers have a problem. At the price you are charging, kids want more lemonade than you have. The demand for lemonade is greater than the supply that you can sell. That means that not all the customers who are waiting in line will get the lemonade that they want. What do the customers do when supply is low?

Seeing that your supply is low, some customers may be willing to pay more for your lemonade than other customers will. Because some customers are willing to pay more, you might even choose to raise the price for your lemonade.

In other words, sellers know that some buyers will pay more for something than other buyers. Because the demand for your lemonade is so high, people will be willing to pay more for it. When demand is high and supply is low, prices go up.

If the supply of lemons is high, price will be low.

Bad weather can change the price of different fruits.

5. Changes in Supply and Demand

At your lemonade stand, you learned how supply and demand affect the price you sell your lemonade for. In a free market economy, supply and demand affect how the prices for all goods and services change.

Suppose that one year California has freezing weather. The cold spoils half of the year's crop of lemons. The supply of lemons is way down. There aren't enough lemons for everyone who wants them. The farmers know that customers will pay more to get the lemons they want. The farmers decide to raise their prices.

Suppose that the next year, farmers in California have grown a huge crop of lemons. There are more lemons than anyone has seen in years. The supply of lemons is way up. The farmers want to sell all their lemons. The farmers know that customers will buy more lemons if the price is lower, so they lower their prices.

Think about the prices of other things affected by supply and demand. The week before Halloween, lots of people want to buy pumpkins. The demand for pumpkins is higher at this time of year than in any other month. Because demand is going up, prices go up. When Halloween is over, demand goes back down. Farmers lower their prices so they can sell their pumpkins.

Pumpkins often cost less after Halloween.

In a free market economy, prices go up and down because of supply and demand. Knowing what price they can sell their goods and services for helps people earn money.

Lesson Summary

In a free market economy, people can choose how they want to earn money. They can choose to provide a service, or they can choose to make a good. People can also choose to work for a business. Businesses can also make many choices about how they want to earn money. Incentives and changes in laws can affect the choices that businesses make.

Buyers and sellers, through supply and demand, affect prices in a free market economy. High supply and low demand lead to lower prices. Low supply and high demand lead to higher prices. When either supply or demand changes, prices change, too.

Becoming an Entrepreneur

Many people want to create their own businesses. However, starting a business can be challenging. You'll read about two people who overcame obstacles and worked hard to make their businesses successful.

One person who created her own business is Oprah Winfrey. She was born in a small town in Mississippi. As a child, Oprah was very poor. She often had to wear homemade overalls made of old potato sacks to school. She also had a doll made from an old corn cob to play with.

When Oprah was young, many people thought she was a very good speaker. She even practiced interviewing her doll.

Oprah Winfrey started her own business in entertainment.

After winning a contest, Oprah went on the radio. The radio station had her read the news. The people at the radio station liked her so much that they offered her a job as a news reporter.

Oprah worked for many different news shows over the next few years. But sometimes she cried on camera when the news was sad. The news shows did not like that she did this.

But Oprah was determined to work on television. When she got a job on a morning talk show, she finally found what she wanted to do. The morning show became very popular, and within a few years, Oprah was offered her very own talk show.

Harpo Studios, which makes television shows, is a part of Oprah's business.

Oprah didn't stop once she got her talk show. Instead, Oprah decided to be an **entrepreneur,** or someone who takes risks to start a business. She created her own company called Harpo Productions. This company created magazines, television programs, movies, and even a television station.

Oprah became very successful and wealthy. Some entrepreneurs choose to use their wealth to start a **charity.** Oprah started a charity that has helped people in need around the world. Her money has gone to opening new schools and helping people who have been affected by natural disasters.

entrepreneur someone who helps start and manage a new business

charity a group that helps raise money for people who need it

Bill Gates

Bill Gates is another entrepreneur. Unlike Oprah, Bill Gates grew up in a wealthy family. He lived in Seattle, Washington, with his parents and two sisters.

Bill loved to read, and he did very well in school. One year, a company in Seattle let his school use its computers. Bill became very interested in computers and what they could do. He spent his free time working on the computer and even made a program so that people could play tic-tac-toe on it.

At school, Bill met a boy named Paul Allen. They bonded over their interest in computers and even helped fix the school's computer programs. They also worked on creating their own program that checked traffic. Bill and Paul sold this program to the city of Seattle for $20,000.

Bill Gates created a business that makes programs for computers.

While at college, Bill continued to work on computers. After creating a program for a new personal computer, Bill and Paul decided to create their own company called Microsoft.

At first, Bill had some trouble. Many people used the program that he had worked on without paying for it. But Bill didn't give up. He created new programs and continued to work on making Microsoft better. Within five years of forming Microsoft, the company was worth millions of dollars. Today, Microsoft is a very large company that has made billions of dollars.

Bill and his wife, Melinda, created a charity called the Bill and Melinda Gates Foundation. They now give money to help many people in need. Entrepreneurs like Bill Gates and Oprah Winfrey not only created their own businesses, but they also help make important changes to people's lives. ◆

Microsoft has made billions of dollars since Bill Gates created it.

Using Money Wisely

Why do we save money?

Introduction

Do you do chores at home? If you do, your family may give you an allowance. What would you do with this money you earn?

Some people decide to spend the money they earn right away. They might go to the store and buy a snack or a small toy. But other people choose to save the money that they have earned.

People choose to save money for many reasons. Some people choose to save money in case of an emergency. Others save money because they want to buy something in the future.

Businesses may also choose to save money. Many businesses save money by finding ways to spend less on the goods that they create. They can use the money they save to move to a bigger factory or buy new machines.

People and businesses save money for many reasons. In this lesson, you will explore why and how people and businesses save their money.

◀ It is important for people to save money. This girl is bringing the money she has saved to the bank.

Social Studies Vocabulary

interest

invest

$ Economics

If you want to buy a video game system, you will need to save money.

1. People Save Money

For many people, saving money is not as fun as spending it is. You can choose to spend your money to buy a cookie that you can eat and enjoy right away.

You may also choose to not buy the cookie. Instead, you could choose to put that money aside and save it for later. Why do people choose to save their money rather than spend it?

Many people save so that they can buy something that costs more money than they have right now. Suppose you want to buy a new video game system. But video game systems are expensive. In order to buy the system, you would need to save some or all of your allowance each week. Saving money allows people to buy things that cost more money.

Another reason that people save money is because they do not know what will happen to them in the future. Suppose that you are riding your bike. Suddenly, your bike gets a flat tire. If you have money saved up, you could buy a new tire right away. If not, you won't be able to ride your bike. Saving allows people to pay for things when accidents happen.

Your parents can also save money for you. Some parents put money aside for when you are old enough to go to college. Doing well in school, even in elementary school, is important. At school, you gain new knowledge and skills. You can use this knowledge and these skills in your life. As you learn more skills at school, you have more opportunities to get better jobs in the future. The money your parents save for you allows you to learn more things later on.

You can use the money that you save to fix your bike.

2. Ways People Save Money

If you want to save your money, where would you put it? There are many different ways that people choose to save their money.

At home, you can put extra money you have in a jar or a piggy bank. You can use the money you save in the piggy bank to buy something you like in the future.

Piggy banks are a good way to save small amounts of money. Because you can keep a piggy bank at home, you can easily put more money in it. But if you have a piggy bank at home, your money could get lost or even stolen. You may not want to save your money in a piggy bank. Where can you store your money so that it will be safe?

Some people save their money in a piggy bank.

Many people choose to save their money in a bank. A bank is a place where people can store their money safely. If you want to save your money in a bank, your parents can open a savings account for you.

Banks offer **interest** on money that you save in your bank account. Suppose you deposit $100 into your savings account at the bank. A year later, you go back to see how much money you have saved. You may be surprised to see that your savings account now has $101. That extra $1 is interest that you earned by saving money at a bank. The more money you store in a bank, the more money you can earn from interest.

The government also protects money in banks. If a bank closes or is robbed, the government will make sure that you do not lose your money.

People can save their money at a bank.

interest extra money that you make from saving money at a bank

This man is using a machine that helps him make shoes quickly.

3. Businesses Use Their Money Wisely

Businesses also save money. But where does this extra money come from?

When a business earns a profit, it can choose to put that money back into the business or save some of that profit to use later. Businesses can find ways to spend less on the things they make. They can choose to save this extra money.

One way that a business can spend less money is by using machines. Machines can make goods quickly. By using machines, a business needs less time and money to make a good. For example, it may take one worker a whole day to make a pair of shoes by hand. But with a machine, the same worker can make thousands of shoes in a day. The business needs fewer employees to make shoes. It spends less money because it no longer needs to pay as many workers to make shoes.

Businesses can also spend less money by choosing different resources to use. Sometimes a business might find that they can make their goods with cheaper resources.

One type of resource is a natural resource. Natural resources are things that can be found in nature, like plants. Look at your shirt. Some shirts are made from cotton. Cotton comes from a plant, so shirts made from cotton are made from natural resources. A business may find that cotton does not cost as much money as other materials. The business may choose to make shirts out of cotton. It will spend less money on each shirt that it makes. The business saves the money it does not spend.

Cotton is a natural resource that a business can use to make clothing.

4. Businesses Invest Their Money

Spending less money helps businesses of all sizes do well. What can a business do with the money that it sets aside?

Businesses can **invest** the money they set aside. When a business invests its money back into the business, it is trying to make even more money.

One way to make even more money is to buy new machines so that goods are made faster. For example, the owner of a business may already own a machine. But the owner may find that a new machine would help him make twice as many goods as he can now. If he has saved enough money, the owner can invest by buying a new machine. This machine will help the business make more money in the future.

Sometimes machines break down, and a business needs to pay someone to fix it. If the business has saved its money, it can fix the broken machine. When the machine is repaired, the business can continue to make goods to sell.

invest using money in the hopes of making more money in the future

This man is a fixing a broken elevator so that people can use it.

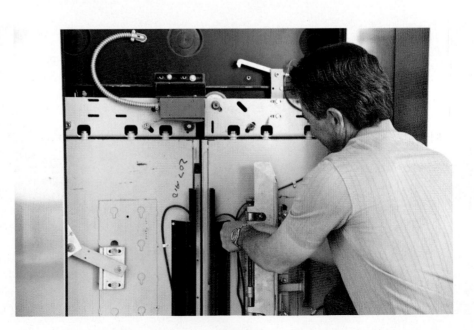

Businesses save their money so that they can invest in creating new things to sell. In a free market economy, businesses compete with one another by inventing new and useful goods or services.

Do you have a computer at home? Many different businesses make computers and compete with one another to get people to buy their goods. They often spend money each year to invent new ways to make their computers better and faster.

If businesses save, they can spend that money to invent new ways to make their goods better. Businesses save money so that they can make better goods to sell to their customers.

Companies invent new things to make computers better and faster.

Lesson Summary

Many people choose to save their money instead of spending it. People save their money so that they can buy something expensive in the future, or they can put money aside in case they need to fix something that breaks. They can save this money in a bank.

Businesses save money by finding ways to spend less on making goods. They can choose to use machines or choose cheaper resources. They then can save this money for new machines or to invent new things.

Economics

Creating a Budget

People do not have enough money to buy everything that they want. We all have to plan how we will spend the money that we have. How can we create a plan for how to spend our money?

Mr. Bessie's class had worked very hard this year. Each student had studied very hard, and they had all done really well on the tests. Mr. Bessie decided that his class would have a party to celebrate how well they had done that year.

The class seemed excited about celebrating. Each student wanted to have different things at the party. Some students wanted to have lots of snacks and a very large cake. Others wanted to fill the room with balloons and confetti. One student even wanted a piñata. Mr. Bessie told each student to bring $5 to class.

Students vote on how they want to spend their party money.

The next day, all twenty students brought money to class. All together, they had $100. The students voted on how to spend the money. They decided that they wanted to buy balloons, board and card games, some snacks and drinks, and fun music to listen to.

The class voted on all the things they wanted to buy with their money.

After the class decided what they wanted, Mr. Bessie helped the class make a **budget**. A budget is a plan for how to spend and save money. First, he created a list of all the things that the students agreed on buying. The class talked about how much money they should spend on each thing on the list.

The class voted to spend $10 on balloons, $20 on snacks and drinks, $30 on board games, and $10 dollars on music. After they voted, the class still had $30 left over. They decided that they should save $10 in case they needed something extra to buy.

Mr. Bessie suggested that they **donate,** or give, the remaining $20 to charity. The class chose to give the money to their local animal shelter. With the $20 they donated, the shelter could buy food for the animals it took care of.

budget a plan for how to use money

donate give money or goods to someone in need

The class had to choose which games they could buy with the money from the budget.

Mr. Bessie and the students went to the store to buy the supplies. Mr. Bessie broke the students up into different groups. Each group was in charge of finding one thing on the list.

One group of students was sent to find balloons for the party. They found that the store sold different types of balloons in many sizes and colors. The students wanted to buy the big balloons, but found that the big balloons cost $12. The cost of big balloons was too high for their budget. The bag of small balloons only cost $8, so the students chose to buy the bag of small balloons instead.

Another group was sent to find board games. There were many types of board games, but they could not buy all of them. The students only had $30, so they chose to buy two board games.

The students were very happy with their shopping trip. Each group of students had made careful choices about what to buy. By the end of their shopping trip, the class hadn't spent all of their money. They still had an extra $15 to save. With the $10 they planned to save, the class now could save $25.

When they got back to class, the students set up the party. All the students had a fun time.

The class decided that they could save the money left from their budget for something else in the future. Maybe they could even donate the money to Mr. Bessie's class next year. That way the next class could have an even bigger party. ◆

The students were able to have the party that they wanted by making a budget.

ITEM	BUDGET	AMOUNT SPENT
Balloons	$10	$8
Board Games	$30	$25
Drinks and Snacks	$20	$15
Music	$10	$7
Money to Donate	$20	$20
Money to Save	$10	$10
Total	$100	$85

$15 Under Budget

Mr. Bessie's class used a table to keep track of the budget.

The United States and Global Trade

How does global trade affect our economy?

Introduction

How many countries does it take to get you to school in the morning? The alarm you use to wake up may be from South Korea. You may get dressed in jeans and a T-shirt that were made in China. When you put on your shoes, you might be putting on something from Thailand.

As part of your breakfast, you could eat a banana that was grown in Ecuador. The orange juice that you drink may be from oranges grown in another part of the United States. When you get a ride to school, it may be in a car designed in Germany. The gas in the car may come from oil found in Canada.

By the time that you arrive at school, you probably have used things that came from many different countries. In this lesson, you will learn how these things get to your community.

Social Studies Vocabulary

global trade
manufactured

◀ The different foods you eat can be from places all around the world.

 Economics   Geography

1. Countries Trade What They Have for What They Want

Have you ever traded things with your friends? Maybe you traded an apple for a banana at lunch. Or maybe you traded a toy for a game. Why did you trade with your friend?

When people trade with one another, they trade things they have for things that they want. Different countries can trade with each other, too. For example, Ecuador is a country that trades with the United States. Ecuador grows lots of bananas. The United States does not grow bananas, but people in the United States want to eat them. So the United States buys bananas from Ecuador.

Bananas from Ecuador can be traded for tractors from the United States.

What does Ecuador want? Farmers in Ecuador need tractors. The United States has many factories that make tractors. So Ecuador buys tractors from the United States.

Ecuador sells bananas to the United States. The United States sells tractors to Ecuador. You could say that Ecuador trades its bananas for tractors. In the same way, the United States trades its tractors for bananas.

These kinds of trades go on all over the world. Countries have traded with one another for hundreds of years. This is called **global trade**. Today, global trade is bigger than ever before. One reason for this is that people have figured out better ways to move and store goods.

As global trade grows, countries around the world rely on each other more and more. The United States wants bananas, and Ecuador has more bananas than it wants. Ecuador wants more tractors, and the United States has more tractors than it wants. The United States and Ecuador can now trade with one another, and both countries are better off.

Many goods travel on container ships like this one.

global trade the buying and selling of goods and services between countries around the world

Oil drills help dig up oil for people to use.

2. Countries Trade Natural Resources

Countries have different natural resources. They trade resources that they have for ones that they need or want.

Bananas are an example of a natural resource that can be found in Ecuador. They grow best in hot and wet countries, like Ecuador. That's why Ecuador has lots of bananas to sell. The United States buys most of its bananas from countries like Ecuador.

Oil, gold, and copper are also resources. The United States has a large supply of oil, copper, and gold, but people still want to have more. So it buys these resources from other countries. For example, Saudi Arabia has lots of oil. South Africa has many gold and diamond mines. Chile sells more copper than any other country in the world. The United States buys resources from all these countries. In return, it sells the countries things that they want.

The United States has its own resources to sell. For example, wheat grows very well in parts of the United States. The United States can grow and sell lots of wheat to other countries that want it.

Sometimes natural resources can only be found at certain times of the year. Grapes need warm weather to grow. During the summer, the United States produces lots of grapes. It doesn't need to buy grapes from other places. The United States even sells some of its summer grapes to other countries. But during the winter, the United States has to buy grapes from warmer countries, such as Chile and Mexico. Global trade lets people in the United States enjoy grapes all year.

Many of our grapes, like these, come from Chile.

This car is sold in the United States, but it was designed in Germany.

manufactured
made with machines

3. Countries Trade Goods That They Make

In addition to natural resources, countries also trade goods that they make. Some of these goods are made by hand. People make jewelry, clothing, or art that they can trade with people in other countries.

Countries can also trade **manufactured** goods, or goods made in factories. Cars, watches, and shoes are all made in factories. Can you think of other examples?

Why do countries trade for goods that are made somewhere else? One reason is that some countries are known for their high-quality goods. Switzerland is famous for its fine watches. Many people like to buy phones made in South Korea. Germany and the United States design many different types of cars. Some companies in the United States are also known for making very good computers.

A country can also trade for goods that are made someplace else so that it can save money. Some countries can make goods for less money than other countries can. For example, many Chinese businesses make clothes at a low cost. These businesses often pay their workers less money than businesses in the United States do. These businesses can also purchase materials at a cheaper price. Cheaper labor and materials lower the price of the clothes made in China.

Other countries buy these goods because of their low price. This is one reason your jeans, T-shirts, and athletic shoes may come from countries in Asia.

These people are making clothes in a factory in Asia.

4. Business and Global Trade

Global trade has led companies to begin selling their goods in places around the world. Businesses have also changed the way they make and sell goods changes, too.

You could choose to buy clothes made by an American company. But when you check your clothing's tag, you may find that it was actually made in a country on the other side of the world. Why does this American company choose to make your clothes in another country?

Some American companies find that they can make more profit by building factories in other countries . In some countries, materials are cheaper and workers are not paid as much as they are in the United States. Because production costs are lower, businesses save money when making goods.

Labels, like these, tell us where the things we buy are made.

Many times, businesses open stores in other countries so that they can sell their goods to more people. For example, there are many businesses that started in the United States. If these businesses want to sell goods to people in other countries they may open stores in other countries.

Starbucks is an American company, but they opened many stores around the world, like this one in India.

One reason companies can be found around the world is because of changes in the way people communicate. In the past, company owners could not easily talk to their workers if a factory was far away from them. Today, phones allow people to easily talk to people around the world. Companies that are in the United States can easily tell people in a factory in another country what to do. Because of this, many businesses have shops and factories in many different countries.

5. Benefits and Costs of Global Trade

There are many benefits for countries that trade with other countries. Global trade also has many costs as well.

What are some of the benefits? Global trade allows people to buy things from all over the world. It allows people to buy quality goods and goods that are low-cost. Without global trade, you would not be able to have bananas for breakfast all year long, and the prices of the things we want, like clothes, shoes, and cars, would go up.

What are some of the costs? Global trade allows companies to move to countries where they can pay their workers less money. Moving factories to other countries can take jobs away from richer countries. It can also keep pay low for workers in poorer countries.

These workers are making cars in Germany.

These people are fighting for American workers who might lose their jobs when companies move to other countries.

Suppose a shoe company in the United States moves its factories to Thailand. What happens? The company saves money, and new jobs become available for the people of Thailand. But American workers who make shoes may lose their jobs.

Also, global trade means that people don't always buy things that are made locally. When shopping for fruit, people often choose to buy bananas from Ecuador. Even though there are costs to global trade, it brings together the people and countries of the world.

Lesson Summary

Global trade connects countries around the world. Countries trade what they have for what they want. They trade natural resources and goods they make. Businesses can also sell different goods or build factories in countries around the world.

Global trade allows people to buy quality and low-cost goods from other places, but some countries may lose businesses and jobs to other countries. In poorer countries, global trade may keep workers' pay low. However, both rich and poor countries are often better because of global trade.

Economics   Geography

How Trade Is Changing Bengaluru

Countries trade resources. They trade goods that they make. Countries also trade services. This kind of trade can bring about big changes in a community. How is the global trade in services changing one city in India?

Suppose that you are writing an e-mail to a friend, and suddenly your e-mail stops working. You might think that you can fix it yourself, but after several minutes, you realize that you cannot do it alone. You need help. At the bottom of the screen, you notice that there is a phone number for the company that runs your e-mail service that you can call if you need help. A young man named Ravi (RAH-vee) answers the phone and helps you fix your e-mail.

Bengaluru is a city in the country of India.

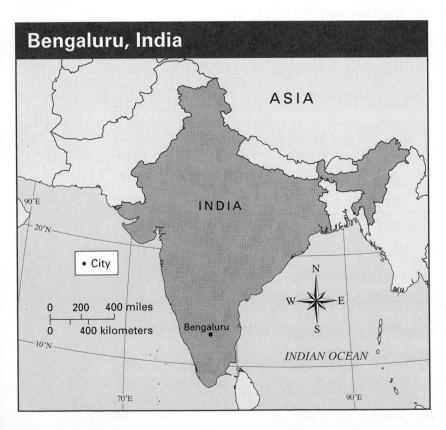

Bengaluru, India

ASIA

90°E

20°N

INDIA

• City

0   200   400 miles

0   400 kilometers

N

W   E

S

Bengaluru

70°E

90°E

10°N

INDIAN OCEAN

Ravi does not live in your town or your state. Ravi does not even live in the United States. He is talking to you from Bengaluru (BEN-guh-luu-roo), India, a place on the other side of Earth. Many U.S. companies have moved some of their work there. As a result, life is changing fast for people who live in Bengaluru, like Ravi.

Why Companies Move Services to Bengaluru

Ravi works in a call center, a place where people help customers who call in about a product. Many U.S. companies have moved their call centers to India. Why? One reason is to save money. Companies do not have to pay workers as much money in India as they do in the United States.

But why do the companies choose Bengaluru? One reason is that the workers in Bengaluru speak English. This means that they can talk to customers in the United States. Also, the city tries to make it easy for companies to move there. For example, it has a school that trains people to work with computers.

Today, Bengaluru is one of India's fastest growing cities. There are lots of new jobs for people like Ravi, but many people's lives are changing as well.

Many companies have moved their call centers to Bengaluru.

How Ravi's Life Is Changing

A year ago, Ravi lived with his parents in the countryside. Most young people in India stay with their families until they are married. Many do not have enough money to live on their own. Then Ravi got his job at the call center, and now he earns enough money to take care of himself. He lives in a new apartment. There are many new apartments being built in Bengaluru. Ravi is still trying to get used to the noise and smell of all the traffic in the city.

When Ravi was little, Bengaluru had about 3 million people. Today, it has about 10 million! About 5 million cars, trucks, and motorcycles creep through the crowded streets. And there are still wooden carts pulled by oxen, too. The carts add to the traffic jams.

Life is changing fast in Bengaluru. Today, the city is a mix of old and new.

Other parts of Ravi's life are changing, too. When Ravi was a boy, he spoke a language called Kannada (KAH-nuh-duh). He learned English to get his job. Now Ravi hears more and more people speaking English around Bengaluru.

Ravi used to go shopping with his family in the markets in the old part of the city. Ravi still likes to touch and taste the fresh fruits and vegetables there. But mostly he goes to fancy stores and shopping malls now. Sometimes he eats at one of the new fast-food restaurants.

Ravi's parents worry about some of the changes they see. They are afraid of losing their old ways of life. "I still like the old ways," Ravi tells them. "But changes are sure to go on. We're part of a much bigger world now, and there is no going back again." ◆

Bengaluru still has its old street markets, but it also has fancy new shopping centers.

Providing Public Services

What different services does our community have?

Introduction

You can find services in your community. Services are tasks that other people do for you. Some businesses sell services to people. They may offer plumbing and cleaning services. Even chefs in restaurants are providing a service. You have to pay to use these services.

Other services are offered to everyone. These are usually provided by a government. Cities, states, and the United States all have their own governments that provide services.

People can use the services a government provides for free or at a low cost. This is because every person in a community helps to pay for these services.

What are some of the services that governments offer? And how do we pay for them? You'll find out in this lesson.

Social Studies Vocabulary

first responder
private service
public service
suburb
tax

◀ Millions of American children get educated in public schools every year. Education is an example of a public service in the United States.

Civics $ Economics

Neighbors allow people to feel accepted.

1. Why We Form Communities

Why do people choose to live together? There are many benefits that come with living in a community.

Living in a community provides people with security. Police and firefighters make sure that citizens are always safe.

In communities, there are different rules and laws. Laws promote safety and make sure that people have the rights they deserve. Citizens come together to make laws.

Communities give people a feeling of acceptance. It feels good to know that there are people who care about you. People in communities become friends with their neighbors and coworkers.

Neighbors make sure to look out for each other. If people have problems, they can go to a neighbor for help.

People can usually find jobs in their community. People need jobs so that they can make a living. They work to make money, which they need to purchase important goods and services.

Communities also give people easy access to services. Individuals can provide **private services** for a community. Getting a haircut at a barber shop is an example of a private service. But a community's government also has **public services** for everyone living there. Some examples of public services are providing clean water and electricity.

private service a service that is provided for money by a business

public service a service, such as a public library, that is offered by a community to everyone

This librarian is making a living and helping his community at the same time.

2. Paying for Public Services

Governments provide public services to communities. However, it costs money to provide these services. How do governments pay for public services?

Public services are paid for with **taxes**. Taxes are money that people and businesses pay to a government. Cities, states, and the United States all have governments. They each collect their own taxes.

There are many different kinds of taxes. One important kind of tax is income tax. This tax is based on how much money someone makes. People who make more money pay more income tax.

tax money that people pay to a government

This man is paying his taxes with the help of a computer and phone.

Another type of tax is sales tax. Sales tax is a fee that is added when people purchase goods and services. For example, when you buy new clothes, you also have to pay the sales tax.

Property taxes are paid by people who own land. All homeowners have to pay property taxes. People who rent their apartment or home do not need to pay a property tax.

Taxes pay for the public services that communities use every day. Communities and their leaders come together to discuss taxes. They talk about what goods and services they want to be public services. Next, you will learn some of the public services that are available in many communities.

This family is looking to buy new clothes. They will need to pay sales tax in addition to the price of the clothes.

This police officer has pulled a driver over for not following the rules of the road.

3. Police

All communities need to keep the peace. Providing this service is the job of the police.

Police keep the peace in several ways. They make sure that people obey laws. For example, police give tickets to drivers who don't stop at red lights. Police walk or ride through neighborhoods to make sure people are safe. They arrest people who steal or commit other crimes.

Police also help people in other ways. They direct traffic and give directions to people who are lost. They help rescue people when floods, earthquakes, and other disasters happen.

Police around the United States are alike in many ways. However, they are also different. Some police ride in police cars. Others ride motorcycles, bicycles, and even horses. Some police officers patrol the highways, while others focus on protecting people and their neighborhoods.

Many police officers are heroes in their communities. In 2012, one officer from West Covina, California, saved a choking baby before catching a bank robbery suspect 30 minutes later! The officer got a 911 call saying a young child was having trouble breathing. He saved the baby before catching up to the suspect in a car chase. The officer was awarded a medal from the police department for his actions.

These police officers both work in New York City, but they get around very differently. One rides a horse, while the other uses a motorcycle.

4. Health Care

In the United States, people can get some kinds of health care as a public service. Taxes help to pay for health care for older people and many poor people. Veterans, or former members of the military, along with children can also have some of their care provided for by public services.

There are public hospitals where people can get care for free or at a low cost. Towns and cities may offer other services, such as free flu shots. If people need emergency care, they can get help at a hospital even if they can't pay for it.

This elderly woman is receiving care from her doctor. Older people can receive some types of care as a public service.

But most health care in the United States is a private service. This means that individuals and companies, not the government, run doctor offices and hospitals.

Have you ever needed help from a nurse or a doctor? Nurses and doctors are health care workers. Health care workers take care of people who get hurt or sick. They also try to keep people from getting sick in the first place.

There are also many other jobs in healthcare. Scientists help create medicines to treat the sick. Engineers make equipment for hospitals that doctors need to care for their patients.

Ambulances take people to the hospital when they are sick or in pain.

In kindergarten, children begin learning how to read and to write. Students in public school are using a public service.

5. Public Schools

Do you go to a public school? If so, then you are getting a public service.

Money from taxes pays for public schools. The whole community pays these taxes, not just the families of students.

Public schools do a very important job for the community. Schools teach students many useful skills, such as how to read, write, and do math. Students will need these skills to get good jobs and to be helpful members of the community.

In the United States, you can go to public schools from kindergarten through high school. After high school, you might choose to go to a public college. You would have to pay part of the cost, and taxes would help pay the rest.

You can also go to a private school or college. These schools don't get money from taxes. Instead, they charge students and their families for their services.

Until about 1850, most schools in the United States were private schools. If students didn't have enough money, they didn't go to school. In most places, only boys went to school.

Many things have changed since then. Today, people agree that everyone needs a good education. This agreement is why the government provides schools as a public service.

These students are graduating from high school. They might attend either a public or private college.

6. Fire Fighting

Fire fighting is an important service. Putting out fires takes a lot of skills, training, and courage. Firefighters around the world often risk their lives to do their job.

Many places still use volunteers to fight fires. But towns and cities may hire trained fire fighters as a public service. They also buy equipment for fighting fires.

Firefighters try to keep fires from starting in the first place. They teach people what to do to prevent fires and to make sure that people obey fire safety laws.

Firefighters risk their lives on a daily basis to keep our communities safe.

Firefighters help communities in other ways, too. They help take care of people who are hurt in accidents. They also help people after disasters such as floods and earthquakes.

On September 11, 2011, terrorists crashed two planes into the World Trade Center in New York City. The New York Fire Department, which is a public service, sent firefighters to the World Trade Center. These firefighters were **first responders**. Many of them lost their lives trying to save people from the wreckage. Their acts of courage are still remembered today.

New York City firefighters were first responders to the events of September 11th.

first responder a person trained to give help at the scene of an emergency

The San Francisco cable cars are a form of public transportation. They have been running for over 100 years.

suburb a community that grows up on the edge of a city

7. Public Transportation

In towns and cities around the United States, people need to get from place to place. Governments often try to help by offering public transportation.

Many cities have public buses. Some cities also have streetcars, which are small trains that use city streets. Larger cities often have subways. Subways are trains that run under the ground. Some places have trains and buses that run between cities and the **suburbs**. Suburbs are communities that grow up on the edges of cities.

In most places, you must pay to use public transportation. But the cost is usually low so that most people can afford it.

Public transportation helps people get around without using cars. Most car engines make the air dirty. When there are fewer cars on the street, the air is cleaner.

Many cities are making it easier for people to use bicycles instead of driving cars. In some cities, you can even rent a bicycle for a low cost. Some people ride bikes to get to public buses and trains. Then they park and lock the bikes, or even bring them along for the ride.

This man is using both his bicycle and public transportation to get around.

8. Public Parks

Have you ever played in a public park? If you have, then you have used a popular public service.

Why do governments spend tax money on parks? Parks bring us many benefits. They add beauty and a touch of nature to our cities and towns. Parks also give us space for all kinds of activities.

Imagine spending a sunny Saturday afternoon in a large city park. You see families having picnics and people walking their dogs. Skaters scoot along the park's paths. You see a softball game and a soccer match. You pass a band playing on an outdoor stage while people dance. In a playground area, parents talk while their children play on the swings and slides. On a pretty lake, people are rowing boats. Where else in a city can people do so many fun and healthy things?

Public parks provide a place for people to run and to play.

Parks are useful for another reason. They bring people together and help create good feelings in a community. Some parks even have community gardens. There, neighbors can work side by side growing flowers, herbs, fruits, and vegetables.

Community gardens provide neighbors a place to work together.

Lesson Summary

There are many reasons why people live in communities. One of them is that communities offer public services. Governments raise money for these services by collecting taxes. Cities, states, and the United States all have their own taxes.

Police and firefighters keep people safe. Health care services help people who are sick or hurt. Public schools teach students skills they need to get good jobs in the future. Public transportation helps people get from place to place without using cars. Parks give people places to play and to enjoy nature. What are the public services where you live?

Civics History

Benjamin Franklin, Public Servant

Today, we count on many public services, but, long ago, towns and cities had few services. What famous American helped to start some needed public services? And how else did he help his city and his country?

Suppose a young newspaper writer is sitting at a table in the city of Philadelphia in 1788. The writer is a little nervous because he is about to interview one of the most famous Americans in the world: Benjamin Franklin.

Franklin is 82 years old and has a friendly twinkle in his eyes. The writer thinks, "Maybe I shouldn't be so nervous after all!"

Let's listen as the interview begins.

Here, Franklin, a popular figure across America, is being cheered by the people of Philadelphia.

Benjamin Franklin spent time as a volunteer firefighter. Volunteer firefighters made Philadelphia a safer place to live.

Writer: Sir, you are a hero to the readers of my newspaper. They would like to know more about your life.

Franklin: I would be happy to talk to your readers. You know, I used to print my own newspapers.

Writer: When did you first come to Philadelphia?

Franklin: I came here in 1723 at the age of 17. I went to work in a printer's shop. I had learned about the business from my brother James. Soon, I owned my own shop.

Writer: Even as a young man, you solved problems in the city. What were some of them?

Franklin: One major problem was fire. Everyone used candles for light and coal for heat, and most houses were made of wood. Naturally, fires started and spread easily. I helped to start a group of volunteer firefighters. Soon other groups of firefighters started in the city. Philadelphia became a much safer place because of the firefighters.

Benjamin Franklin printed this 20 shilling bill while he worked in a printer's shop. Shillings were the form of money used in the colonies.

Benjamin Franklin helped start the Pennsylvania Hospital in Philadelphia for the treatment of poor people.

Writer: What were some other problems?

Franklin: Well, the streets were dirty and dark. I began a program to clean them up and add lights. Also, many sick people were poor and were having trouble getting the care they needed. I raised money for a city hospital that helped treat people who could not normally afford care.

Writer: In 1775, the war for independence from Great Britain began. Why did you get involved?

Franklin: To protect our rights! We wanted to make our own laws and vote on our own taxes. But Britain would not let us, so I knew we had to fight. In 1776, I even helped to write the Declaration of Independence.

Writer: But what if Britain had won the war? Then people like you would have been hanged as rebels!

Franklin: That is why we Americans had to help one another. We had to hang together, or we surely would have hanged separately!

Writer: In 1776, you were sent to France on behalf of the American people. Why?

Franklin: We needed France's help to win the war. I went there to ask the king for soldiers and money to buy supplies.

Writer: Wasn't it dangerous to sail to France in the middle of a war?

Franklin: Oh, yes, the risk of going was huge. The British could have captured our ship, and we would have been hanged for sure! But it all turned out well. We did win the war—with France's help. And we made a new country based on the ideas of liberty and equality.

Writer: Many people say you are a wise man. What advice would you give other Americans?

Franklin: Don't think only of yourself, but instead think about what you can do for others. Work for the good of your community and your country. It is better to be useful than to be rich. ◆

Benjamin Franklin is seen here at the Palace of Versailles in France. Franklin was trying to convince the King of France to help America in its battle for independence.

Government in the United States

How is our government set up?

Introduction

Does your community have a city hall? Maybe it's called a town hall where you live. This building is where your community's government has its offices. There you'll find the people who keep your city or town running smoothly.

These people have many duties. Some of them make laws. Others make sure that the parks are clean or that streetlights are working.

In this lesson, you'll learn about a community's government. You'll visit a city called Pleasantville. You'll meet the people who work in Pleasantville's city hall and find out what they do.

Cities and towns aren't the only places with governments. Your state also has a government, and so does our country. Each level of government has a job to do. You'll learn how each level of government helps us meet our needs.

> ### Social Studies Vocabulary
>
> **city hall**
> **Constitution**
> **federal government**
> **legislature**
> **local government**
> **public works**
> **state government**

◀ City leaders help run New York City's local government.

 Civics

Does your community have a city hall?

local government
the government of a city, town, county, or other area in the United States that is smaller than a state

city hall the building where the offices of a community's government are located

1. The Mayor and the City Council

Welcome to the city of Pleasantville! Like most cities and towns, the people who live here elect leaders to run the government. In Pleasantville, voters elect a mayor and a city council. The mayor is the head of the city council.

The mayor and the city council of Pleasantville are part of the **local government**. They work at **city hall** and try to make the city a safe and fun place to live. Their most important job is to make laws for the city. Laws tell people what they can do and cannot do. In Pleasantville, one law says people must clean up after their pets. Another law says how fast people can drive near a school.

Many other workers help the mayor and the city council. The police help make sure that people obey the law. Firefighters help keep people safe. People in other departments have their own special work to do.

All these people need money to do their jobs. The money comes from taxes. The mayor and the city council know how much money there is to spend. They decide how much money to give to each part of the city's government.

The city council holds meetings. It decides how much money to give each part of the government.

2. The City Manager

The mayor and the city council make many decisions. They need someone to make sure their decisions are carried out. In Pleasantville, this is the job of the city manager.

Suppose the city council decides to have a Kids' Day. The city manager would be in charge of planning this special day. If you wanted to help with the celebration, then you would talk to the city manager.

The city manager makes sure the city's work gets done.

The city manager has other duties, too. One is to make a detailed budget for how to spend the city's money. Another duty is to think of ways to make the city a better place to live. The city manager tells these ideas to the mayor and city council.

The city clerk keeps records for the city.

3. The City Clerk

A city clerk keeps records for a community. In Pleasantville, the city clerk keeps records of births and deaths. The city clerk also takes notes during city council meetings. Anyone can read the notes so that people always can know what the council is doing.

The city clerk takes care of many other kinds of documents, too. Suppose a family wants to add a room to its house. To do this, the family needs to get a document called a permit from the city clerk.

Another important job is to help run the city's elections. The city clerk keeps records of elections and helps make sure that election laws are obeyed.

The parks and recreation department is in charge of the city's parks and playgrounds.

4. The Parks and Recreation Department

Pleasantville has many parks and playgrounds. It also has a public swimming pool and a city golf course. The city's parks and recreation department is in charge of these places.

Sometimes a playground needs a new slide. People might want a bike path in a city park. The showers at the public swimming pool might need to be fixed. The parks and recreation department takes care of these things.

The department also plans fun things for people to do. It organizes softball teams, offers swimming lessons, and even sets up community gardens around town.

5. The Public Library

Most towns and cities have public libraries. Libraries are good places to go when you want information or something fun to read. You can find many books, magazines, and newspapers there.

In Pleasantville, people use public libraries in many ways. They borrow books to read at home and use the computers to go on the Internet. They also use materials in the libraries to learn more about their local area.

The city's libraries are good for other things, too. They have story times for children. Sometimes they show movies or have concerts. They have reading groups that people can join. Sometimes writers visit to talk about their books.

Public libraries provide information and entertainment.

6. The Fire Department

Pleasantville has its own fire department. The fire department has two main jobs. The first job is to help people in emergencies. The city's firefighters don't just put out fires. They also help to rescue people from dangerous situations and give medical care to people who are hurt.

The second job is to teach people what to do in an emergency. The fire department shows schools and offices how to have fire drills. Fire drills help people know what to do if a fire breaks out. The fire department also sends speakers to schools. The speakers tell students what to do in a serious situation, such as an earthquake or a flood.

When a fire happens, the fire department tries to find out how it started. This helps firefighters learn more about how to prevent fires in the future.

The fire department helps to keep people safe from fires and other dangers.

7. The Police Department

Pleasantville has a large police department. The police help to keep people safe in two main ways.

First, the police try to make sure people obey the laws. They give tickets to people who drive too fast and try to catch people who steal or commit other crimes.

Second, the police try to stop crimes before they happen. They walk or drive through the city's neighborhoods. They want people to know they are nearby. People feel safer when they know the police are protecting them.

The police also talk to people about how to prevent crimes. They visit neighborhood groups and schools to talk about what the police do and how people can stay safe.

The police department helps to keep people safe from crime.

The planning department makes sure that new buildings fit the city's plan.

8. The Planning Department

Cities and towns are always changing. People want to build new houses and shopping malls. They want new parks and playgrounds. Someone needs to decide which changes are best. In Pleasantville, this is the job of the planning department.

The planning department divides the city into areas called zones. Some zones are for houses, some are for businesses, and some zones are for a mix of both.

The planning department gives permission for new buildings to be built. It makes sure that the idea for a new building matches the city's plan. For example, the building should not cause too much traffic in a neighborhood. It also should fit in well with other buildings nearby.

9. The Public Works Department

Like many other cities and towns, Pleasantville has a **public works** department. Public works are things the city builds for everyone's use, such as roads, water pipes, and streetlights. The department's main job is to keep public works in good shape.

People in the public works department pave roads. They fix broken streetlights and leaks in water pipes. They also build new public works. Suppose the city needs new traffic lights or sewers. First, the mayor and city council vote to spend money on these projects. Then, the public works department does the work.

public works things such as roads, water pipes, and streetlights that everyone in a community uses

Fixing traffic lights is one of the jobs of the public works department.

10. Your State's Government

Pleasantville's government has many parts to keep the city running smoothly. Your local government does, too! But states also need to be run, which is why each state in the United States has its own government.

Each state has a state constitution. This document sets up the **state government**. It describes each part of the state's government.

In each state, people elect a governor to help lead the state. The governor proposes the state budget, appoints officials, and carries out laws.

The governor works with the state's **legislature** to run the state. The legislature is the part of the government that makes laws. People from communities around the state vote for leaders to be part of the state's legislature.

Your state also has a court system to make decisions about what a law means. Courts make sure that laws affect everyone in the state fairly. Judges may be elected or appointed to a court.

state government the government of one of the states of the United States

legislature the part of the government that makes laws

The people elect the governor of a state. Here, Governor Nikki Haley of South Carolina gives a speech.

VALDOSTA STATE UNIVERSITY

Local governments provide public services to a city or town, but state governments provide services for everyone in the state. People pay taxes to the state to fund these services.

States have an education department. Each state helps provide schools to teach students. States also have colleges and universities.

Like local governments, states have a department to maintain public works. The department builds roads that cross the entire state to connect cities and towns. It also finds ways to get water to everyone in the state.

States provide many other services, too. Each state has a highway patrol, provides driver licenses, and takes care of state parks.

The state government provides universities for people.

① **Federal government**

㊿ **State governments**

(1,000) **Local governments**

The United States has different levels of government. But all governments have to follow the Constitution.

federal government the national government of the United States

Constitution the document that sets up the basic rules of the United States government

11. Your Country's Government

People in each state have to follow their state's laws. But they also have to follow the laws of the U.S. government.

The U.S. government is called the **federal government**. It makes laws for the whole country. The basic rules of this government are set by the United States **Constitution**. States cannot disobey the Constitution.

The Constitution sets up how the federal government is structured. The government has a president, a legislature, and a court system.

People elect the president. The president leads the country and carries out laws.

People also elect leaders to Congress, which is the federal government's legislature. Congress make laws for the United States.

The highest court in the United States is called the Supreme Court. This court says what federal laws mean.

The postal service is one service provided by the federal government.

Like local and state governments, the federal government also provides public services. These services are available to everyone in the country. People pay taxes to the U.S. government so that it can provide services and protect the nation.

Have you sent mail at the post office or traveled on an interstate highway? If you have, then you have used services provided by the federal government. The military and public broadcasting are some other services the federal government provides.

Lesson Summary

It takes a lot of people to run local governments like a city or town government. In Pleasantville, the mayor and the city council make the big decisions. The city manager sees that these decisions are carried out. Other people at city hall all have their own jobs to do. Together, they help to keep the city running smoothly.

There are different levels of government. A state government runs each state. The federal government runs the whole country.

Civics History

The Constitution Protects Our Rights

Different communities have their own needs. The federal, state, and local governments work together to meet these needs. But all of these governments must obey the United States Constitution. What happens when states don't follow the Constitution?

The Declaration of Independence was signed in 1776.

In 1776, some of our nation's best thinkers gathered in Philadelphia, Pennsylvania. Each of them dipped his pen in ink to sign his name on the Declaration of Independence. By signing this document, they told the world that the United States was its own nation.

The people who signed the Declaration were our Founding Fathers. They became important leaders in the new nation. They had many ideas for how to run the country.

The Founding Fathers met at Philadelphia again in 1787. But this time, they met to put together the United States Constitution, a document that sets the basic rules for the nation. We still use the Constitution today.

The Constitution sets up our country's government so that we have a president, legislature, and court system. It also gives people the power to choose many of their leaders.

Two years after the Constitution was created, ten amendments were added to it. These amendments are called the **Bill of Rights**. The Bill of Rights protects our freedoms. It says that Americans have the freedom to say what they think. Americans may also choose what religion to follow.

The Constitution sets up the basic rules for our government and is the highest law of the land.

The Bill of Rights protects freedom for the states, too. It gives states the power to make any laws that the Constitution does not prohibit. Still, state and local governments must obey the Constitution. It is the highest law in our country.

Each level of government can make laws. But what happens when state or local governments do not obey the Constitution? In this story, you'll read about events that happened in the city of Little Rock, Arkansas.

Bill of Rights a part of the Constitution that protects the rights and freedoms of Americans

Changing State Laws

In 1868, a new rule was added to the Constitution. It said that the states must give all people, white or black, "equal protection of the laws." This means that a law must treat all people fairly.

But for many years, governments in some places did not obey this rule. In Little Rock, Arkansas, for example, white students and black students could not go to the same schools. The state had laws that separated them.

Schools for white students were nicer. They had more school supplies, heated rooms, and bus systems. But schools for black students did not have these things.

This would change in 1954. The U.S. Supreme Court said that the state law that separated students did not give students "equal protection of the laws." The state law did not follow the Constitution.

In some places, it was against the law for black students and white students to go to the same schools.

Trouble in Little Rock

In September 1957, a new school year was about to start at Central High School in Little Rock, Arkansas. But it wasn't like any school year before it.

This year, African American students would be going to Central High for the first time. Many white people in the city were angry about white students and black students going to the same schools.

The governor of Arkansas was a man named Orval Faubus. Governor Faubus was the head of the state government. He was against black students attending school in Little Rock. He even warned that "blood will run in the streets" if black students tried to go to Central High. Faubus told the state **militia** to prevent the students from entering the school. A militia is made up of soldiers who serve in emergencies.

In 1957, white students and black students went to school together for the first time at Central High School.

militia an army made up of soldiers who serve during emergencies

The first black students at Central High faced angry crowds.

Going Against the Constitution

On September 4, nine black students walked toward Central High. Hundreds of angry white people stood around the school.

Bravely, the nine students kept on walking. Then the state militia blocked their way. Governor Faubus had told the soldiers to keep these students out of the school.

The governor has control over the state militia, but he couldn't go against the federal government. It is a court's job to say what laws mean. One court declared that using the state militia to stop black students from going to school is against the Constitution.

A judge ordered Governor Faubus to let the students into the school. The governor sent the soldiers away.

The President Takes Action

A few weeks later, the black students tried to enter the school again. This time, an even bigger crowd was waiting. Little Rock's city police led the students in through a side door.

The mayor of Little Rock knew that people were still very angry. He was afraid someone might get hurt. He asked U.S. president Dwight Eisenhower for help.

The president is part of the federal government. Usually, keeping the peace is the job of the local government. But the students' rights under the Constitution were in danger. This gave the president a reason to act. He sent U.S. Army troops to Little Rock to protect the black students. The students were able to go to school at last.

The story of Little Rock shows an important idea. We have many governments, each with its own job to do. But all of them must obey the Constitution. ◆

President Eisenhower took action when the students' rights under the Constitution were in danger.

U.S. Army troops helped protect the students.

Citizenship and Participation

How do we have a voice in our community?

Introduction

Has your family ever talked about how to spend a weekend or a vacation? Did you get to say what you thought? If so, then you probably felt better about the choice your family made. If not, then your family may have made a decision that you didn't like. Even if we don't get exactly what we want, we all like to have a voice in the decisions that affect us.

The same is true in your town or city. People want to have a voice in the decisions that affect their lives. Many people want to make their voices heard in the federal government as well. They can make their voices heard in many ways, such as voting or attending public meetings. Also, helping to make important decisions in the community is part of being a good citizen. In this lesson, you'll learn about ways to make your voice heard in your community.

Social Studies Vocabulary

ballot
candidate
civil rights
demonstration
peaceful
register
republic

◄ People can make their voices heard in many ways. This image shows a demonstration in front of the Capitol building.

Civics

In order to win, this man must get support from the people that he would represent.

1. People Choose Our Leaders

You know that the United States has a government. But how does that government work?

The United States government is a **republic**. In a republic, the people choose leaders to make decisions for the country. The leaders are chosen in a democratic way. This means that citizens vote for their leaders.

Our government's power comes from the citizens. Citizens have a say in who makes decisions in our government. They consent, or agree, to let leaders run the country.

When members of government are chosen, they represent the people who elected them to office. They may have told these people what they planned to do. Now, they have a responsibility to keep their promises. Most importantly, they must do what is best for the people they represent.

The members of the government aren't the only people who have responsibilities. All citizens have responsibilities, especially those who can vote. U.S. citizens who are at least 18 years old have the right to vote.

The United States relies on its citizens to vote for the leaders of the country. It is important that the voters stay informed on the issues so that they can choose a good person to represent them.

One of the best ways to stay informed is by reading the news. The news brings important information to people. However, sometimes newspapers want you to vote for certain people. It is best to read different newspapers so you can make the best decision for yourself.

Voting gives people a chance to make changes. You might not always like laws that are made, but new leaders are chosen every few years. You can choose to vote for someone new who agrees with you.

Reading the news is a great way to stay informed about the issues in our country.

2. Going to Public Meetings

One way to have a voice in your community is to go to public meetings. Towns and cities have meetings to talk about important decisions. These decisions affect everyone who lives in the community.

Before making decisions, leaders want to know what people think. They ask people to come to public meetings to share their thoughts and ideas. For instance, leaders might call a meeting to talk about traffic safety near schools. The leaders might ask whether the city should put speed bumps on certain streets to slow cars down.

This is a public meeting in New York City.

Anyone can go to a public meeting. You can go just to listen or to share your thoughts on a topic.

If you choose to speak at a public meeting, then the leaders of the meeting may ask you questions. When you are finished, the next person gets to speak.

It can be hard to talk in front of a group. But if you are brave enough, then speaking at a public meeting will give you a voice in your community. You can tell the leaders of your town or city what you think. You can tell your neighbors, too. You might even change people's minds!

Speakers at a public meeting take turns sharing their thoughts.

3. Taking Part in Peaceful Demonstrations

demonstration a gathering of people to show shared feelings or opinions

peaceful done without hurting others or their property

civil rights rights a person has as a citizen

Have you ever seen a **demonstration**? At a demonstration, people gather to show how they feel about an issue. A **peaceful** demonstration can be a good way of making your voice heard. Peaceful means not hurting others or their property.

Peaceful demonstrations let others know about a problem. People carry signs to show how they feel and listen to speeches. They may chant slogans, sing songs, or march in a parade.

In the 1950s and 1960s, there were many demonstrations in the United States about **civil rights**. Civil rights are rights that people have simply because they are citizens. For instance, all adult citizens have the right to vote.

These people are part of a peaceful demonstration.

Why were civil rights a problem in the 1950s and 1960s? At that time, many African Americans were not being given all their rights. For example, in some states, laws made it hard for them to vote.

Many people wanted these laws to change. Thousands of them took part in civil rights marches. These peaceful demonstrations made many Americans think more about civil rights. In time, new laws were passed to help give all citizens their rights.

This civil rights protest in Washington D.C. took place in 1963.

Barack Obama was the first black president of the United States. Here, he gives a speech to voters who support him.

candidate a person who tries to get elected to do a job in government for a community

4. Supporting a Candidate

Candidates are people who run for office. This means they try to get elected to do a certain job in government for the community. For example, several people may want the job of mayor. To run for this office, they become candidates.

People want to vote for candidates who will make their community a better place. So candidates tell people about their ideas. They give speeches and talk to news reporters. They meet voters in public places, such as shopping malls. Sometimes they even visit people's homes. Then voters choose the candidate they like best.

Candidates need lots of help. They can't talk to every voter. They need people to tell friends and neighbors about their ideas. They need money to send voters mail and to pay for ads on television and radio.

If you like a candidate's ideas, then you can help the person get elected. This is another way to have a voice in your community.

There are many ways to support a candidate. You can give money. You can put signs in your windows or in your yard. You can talk to voters. You can help mail letters to voters. On Election Day, you can encourage people to vote.

Supporting a candidate is one way to make your voice heard.

5. Voting

register to sign up to vote

ballot a form on which people mark their votes in an election

Voting is one of the best ways to have a voice in your community. People vote in elections to choose community leaders. They also can vote on ideas for improving their town or city.

When the United States was created, only certain people could vote. A voter had to be a white man who owned land. Over time, more and more people won the right to vote.

There are still a few rules about who can vote. Voters must be at least 18 years old and citizens of the United States. They also must **register,** or sign up, to vote.

People vote by marking a **ballot**. The ballot lists all the candidates and ideas to vote on. After everyone has voted, the ballots are counted to see which candidates and ideas have won.

People must register before they can vote.

These people are voting on Election Day.

Today, some people vote by mail. But most people vote in person on Election Day. They mark their ballots in small booths. The booths keep other people from seeing how they are voting.

Leaders make most of the decisions for a community. But in an election, every voter helps to choose ideas and candidates. In this way, voting gives people a strong voice in their community.

Lesson Summary

The United States government is a republic, which means the people can choose their leaders. These leaders represent the people who elected them and make decisions that are best for the people they represent. U.S. citizens who are at least 18 years old can vote.

You can have a voice in your community in many ways. You can learn about issues and voice your opinions about them. You can attend public meetings. You also can take part in peaceful demonstrations. You can support and help candidates running for a government office.

Making Your Voice Count

Voting gives you a voice in your community and in your country. But voting is more than just marking a ballot. What steps are involved in being a good voter?

Olivia's school was taking part in a national mock election for president of the United States. A mock election is a pretend election held for practice. The election was big news in town.

Outside her classroom, Olivia saw Anna Wong, a reporter from the local television station. She stopped Olivia to ask her questions about the mock election.

"Are you voting in the mock election?" Ms. Wong asked Olivia.

"I sure am!" Olivia answered.

"Voting is a big responsibility," Ms. Wong said. "Can you tell me how you got ready for the election?"

"Sure," Olivia answered.

Olivia tells a reporter about her school's mock election.

"The first step was registering to vote," Olivia explained. "Some students put up signs in the halls reminding everyone to register two weeks before the election. If we signed up by the deadline, we got a special sticker."

"What was the next step?" Ms. Wong asked.

"The second step was research," Olivia answered. "We had to find out what the candidates were like and what they would do if they got elected. So we read about them on the Internet, and we read articles in newspapers.

"We also had Meet the Candidates events, which were cool. One student would play the part of a candidate, while another student would play the part of a reporter and ask questions. The rest of us tried to decide which candidate had the best ideas."

The first step in an election is registering to vote.

Researching candidates helps you make good choices during an election

These students are marking their sample ballots for the mock election.

"It sounds like you really prepared well," Ms. Wong said. "So then were you ready to vote?"

"Not yet," Olivia answered. "The third step was to learn how to mark the ballot. Our teacher gave us sample ballots because voters in real elections get them, too. We used the sample ballots to learn how to mark our choices correctly. I marked my sample ballot today. That way, I'll know just what to do when I get in the voting booth."

Ms. Wong looked surprised. "You even have voting booths?" she asked.

"Sure, we made them out of cardboard and set them up in our classroom," said Olivia. "Hey, I'd better go complete the last step."

"What's that?" asked Ms. Wong.

Olivia grinned. "Voting for president!" she called as she disappeared into her classroom.

Ms. Wong thought about what she would say on the evening news. She would tell people that the students were very excited about voting for president. Even though their votes wouldn't count in the real election, everyone in town would know how the vote came out. In this way, the students would be making their voices heard.

"I'll say something else, too," Ms. Wong thought. "I'll tell people how hard the students worked to get ready for the election. They understand that voting isn't just a right, but it's also a responsibility. It's something we should do with care."

Just then, Olivia came out of the classroom wearing a big sticker that said, "I Voted Today."

"I can't wait until I'm 18," Olivia told her. "Voting today was fun, but one day my vote can help change the country!" ◆

Understanding the voting process now can help you make good decisions in the future.

Protecting the Environment

How can we care for the environment?

Introduction

Think about the things you do every day. You may get a ride to school in a car or on a bus, or you may use products made in factories. How do these activities affect the area around you?

Our everyday activities can affect the environment in bad ways. We need some goods made in factories, but factories can pollute the air around us. We use oil to heat our homes and provide power for the cars that take us places, but sometimes ships can spill oil into the ocean.

The things people do can make the air, water, or soil dirty or unsafe. This is why we need to take care of our environment.

How do we protect the environment? One way is to solve and reduce problems. In this lesson, you will read about how three communities faced pollution problems, and how these communities worked to solve these issues in their environment.

> **Social Studies Vocabulary**
>
> climate change
> toxic waste

◀ Factories can pollute the environment. What can you do to help?

 Civics  Geography

Los Angeles struggles with air pollution. Sometimes the air turns a dirty brown.

1. Air Pollution

Los Angeles is a large city in southern California. Many people who live there use cars to get around and work in factories in the city.

Los Angeles faces a big problem. The city has a lot of air pollution. Some days, the sky turns a dirty brown, and the air has a bad smell.

Because Los Angeles is so big, it has busy roads and freeways for people to get from place to place. But car and truck engines are a major cause of air pollution.

Los Angeles also has a big airport that many airplanes fly in and out of. Airplanes burn lots of fuel during takeoff, which pollutes the air. Factories nearby also send smoke into the air. This makes the problem even worse.

Some kinds of air pollution help to trap heat from the sun. Scientists say that this increases global temperatures and causes **climate change**. Most scientists worry that too much warming will harm the environment in many ways. They say that some crops and other plants might not grow. Some animals might die out. Some places could have more hot spells, less water, and stronger storms.

Millions of people live in Los Angeles. But it is not good to breathe in air pollution. Air pollution is bad for the lungs. So, people looked for ways to clean the air.

One group of third graders even worked to help solve the problem. How did they fight air pollution?

climate change a rise or fall in Earth's temperature over time

People from all over the world come together to discuss the problem of climate change at conferences like this.

2. Tree Musketeers to the Rescue

Some people formed groups that planted trees to fight air pollution. Trees help take smoke and chemicals out of the air.

In 1987, a group of Girl Scouts who lived near Los Angeles met to think of ways to help clean the air. The girls were all in third grade and wanted to help their community.

After thinking about the problem, the girls decided to plant a tree. But they knew that in order to clean up a lot of air pollution, they needed to get other kids to also plant trees.

The girls decided to form a group called the Tree Musketeers. The group began getting more kids in the area involved with planting trees. Before long, the group had planted more than 700 trees.

Planting trees is a good way to help keep the air clean.

Like a healthy young tree, the girls' idea kept growing. As time went on, new kids joined the Tree Musketeers to help the environment. By 2014, more than a million kids had planted almost two million trees around the world!

Trees can also help with climate change. They soak up a gas called carbon dioxide, which is one of the main kinds of pollution that trap the sun's heat. That's why the Tree Musketeers say they are fighting climate change by planting trees.

Today, Los Angeles's air is still polluted, but it is much cleaner than before. The Tree Musketeers along with many others worked together to fight air pollution. Can you think of other ways to fight air pollution?

Trees help to fight climate change by soaking up carbon dioxide.

The *Exxon Valdez* was carrying oil off the coast of Alaska when it struck a reef.

3. A Huge Oil Spill

We use oil to power our cars, buses, and planes. We also use it to heat our homes and produce goods. But if we aren't careful, an oil spill can cause pollution and hurt the environment.

It was just after midnight on March 24, 1989 when a huge oil tanker called the *Exxon Valdez* moved through the waters off the coast of Alaska. A tanker is a ship that carries liquid or gas. The *Exxon Valdez* was almost as long as three football fields. It carried more than 53 million gallons of oil.

Suddenly, disaster struck. The man steering the ship became careless. He failed to keep the tanker in safe shipping lanes. The ship ran into a reef that lay under the water. The reef punched a hole in the ship, and oil began leaking into the water.

Out of 53 million gallons, about 11 million gallons of oil spread through the water. Birds and other animals got covered in oil. The oil ruined their feathers and fur, so they couldn't stay warm. Some of them began to freeze to death.

As the creatures tried to clean themselves, they swallowed some of the oil. The oil poisoned and killed many of them.

People in Alaska were worried and angry. Thick, sticky oil coated about 1,300 miles of the Alaska shore. Thousands of birds and other animals were sick and dying.

"What can we do about this?" people asked. "And how can we make sure it never happens again?"

Workers had to clean away oil that covered the nearby beaches.

4. Stopping Oil Spills

After the oil spill, people did their best to clean up the mess. Rescuers rushed to save birds and other animals. Thousands of workers began trying to clean up the water and beaches.

But nothing could solve all the problems caused by the oil spill. The spill killed about 250,000 seabirds and 3,000 otters. About 300 seals and about 13 killer whales died. Some of the oil can still be found in the water and on beaches today.

The best solution to oil spills is to keep them from happening in the first place. So the U.S. government took action. It passed a law saying that oil tankers in Alaska must have stronger walls.

Workers tried to save the animals that had been affected by the spill.

Other laws were passed to make sure companies and their workers act more safely. The government also punished the company that owned the tanker. The company agreed to pay millions of dollars in fines. Some of the money helped to pay for the cleanup.

The ship's captain was punished, too. He had to pay a fine of $50,000 and spend many hours helping the affected communities.

Communities in Alaska are doing their part. Today, they are ready to help clean up if another big oil spill happens there. But everyone hopes it never happens again. What other ways are there to prevent oil spills from happening?

Laws have been passed asking oil workers like these to work safely to help prevent accidents.

Scientists test soil for toxic chemicals.

5. Schools and Toxic Waste

A few people in Marion, Ohio became very sick. They had a rare kind of cancer.

As it turns out, all of the people who got sick went to River Valley High School. Soon, others who also went to that school were diagnosed with cancer.

Some people began to wonder why so many people in Marion had cancer. They wondered if something at the high school was causing people who had been students there to get sick.

Many family members of those who were sick joined a group called Concerned River Valley Families. The group demanded that scientists test the school grounds.

It turned out that the soil under the high school contained **toxic waste**. The word *toxic* means "poisonous." *Waste* means "trash" or "garbage."

toxic waste
poisonous trash or garbage

The toxic waste in Marion came from the U.S. Army. Years before, the army had used the land as a place to dump chemicals. The school was built right on top of this toxic waste dump.

At first the army said the land was safe. So did the government of Ohio. The scientists said they didn't know what caused the kind of cancer the people had, so the toxic waste couldn't be blamed.

The parents in the Concerned Families group disagreed. They said they could not take chances with their children's health. They also said that the school was not safe.

Even if this barrel of waste is buried, it can still make the land unhealthy for people living near it.

6. Making Sure Schools Are Safe

The Concerned River Valley Families wanted to close the high school. They talked to the people in charge of the school. They went to public meetings. They made sure that news reporters wrote about the problem.

Thanks to these families, the story made news around the country. Lois Gibbs even came to visit. Do you remember her? She was the mother who spoke up about the dangerous chemicals at Love Canal.

In the end, the families won their fight. The high school was closed, and a new school was built in another location.

Did toxic waste cause those people from River Valley High School to get cancer? No one knows for sure. But many scientists say that toxic waste is especially dangerous to growing children. For this reason, many people want to make sure that schools are safe from toxic chemicals.

Roxanne Krumanaker was one of the parents who fought to close River Valley High School.

Students can help protect the environment and keep their communities safe.

Around the country, parents are taking action. They have stopped some schools from being built on old garbage dumps. They have worked to close schools where dangerous chemicals have been found. And they have demanded new laws to protect children from toxic waste.

These parents are a lot like the Tree Musketeers. They think that pollution is everyone's problem. And they think that everyone can be part of the solution.

Lesson Summary

Some everyday activities people do can harm the environment. It is important for people to get around and use goods from factories, but cars and factories can create pollution.

Many different people have tried to solve or help reduce pollution problems. The Tree Musketeers planted trees in Los Angeles to fight air pollution. The government and local communities have worked to lessen the harm on the ocean caused by oil spills. Parents in Ohio worked to close a school that was built on a toxic waste dump. What might you do to help solve a pollution problem where you live?

Geography

Finding New Sources of Energy

Fighting pollution is one way to help the environment. Another way is to find new sources of energy. Where do we get the energy that lights our homes and fuels our cars? And how can new sources of energy help our planet?

The teams were ready. The students placed their model cars, which were less than two feet long, behind the starting line.

A loud voice rang out, "On your mark, get set, go!" The race began.

The small cars sped down the racetrack as the students held their breath. Which teams would win awards for building the fastest cars? Which would win for the best designs?

What is special about this car?

Geography

This house uses solar panels to collect energy from sunlight.

All car races are exciting, but this one was special. It was part of the Junior Solar Sprint. Teams of middle school students build model cars that run only on solar energy. This type of energy comes from sunlight. Then the teams race their cars down a track.

Why would students build cars that use energy from the sun? One reason is to have fun. But another reason is to learn about **renewable resources**.

Renewable means that we can get more of something. Some energy comes from renewable resources like sunlight, wind, or water. This kind of resource isn't used up. We can get more of it in a short time because we always have sunlight, wind, and water.

renewable resource
a natural resource, such as sunlight, that does not get used up

Why is getting energy from renewable resources important? Humans use lots of energy every day. Energy keeps our houses warm in winter and cool in summer. Energy lights our rooms and runs our computers and televisions. It fuels our cars, buses, and airplanes.

We get most of this energy from sources that lie under the ground, like coal, oil, and natural gas. These resources are called **fossil fuels**. Fossil fuels come from the fossils, or remains, of plants and animals. These remains have been buried in Earth for millions of years.

Someday we will use up these resources. So they are called **nonrenewable resources**. These resources cannot be made again in a short time. Because of this, we need more energy sources.

Coal must be dug out of the ground.

Burning fossil fuels adds pollution to the air.

There is a second reason to find new energy sources. Coal, oil, and gas must be burned to make power. Burning fossil fuels can make the air unhealthy to breathe and puts more carbon dioxide in the air. Carbon dioxide can also increase the global temperature.

Using energy from sunlight, wind, and water doesn't pollute the air. But getting this energy is challenging. Right now it's very expensive to turn these forms of energy into power we can use. But scientists are always looking for ways to get more energy from renewable resources.

That's why the Junior Solar Sprint is so exciting. Racing model cars is just a first step. Some of these students may become scientists and engineers. One day, they could help to find new ways to bring us the energy we need. ◆

Making a Difference in the World

How can we help the world around us?

Introduction

We are all part of many communities. Some communities are small, like your school. Others are much bigger, like your state and country. The largest community of all is the global community. Everyone on Earth is a member of this community, and so are animals and other living things. We all share our planet's water, air, and soil. We all depend on each other to have healthy and happy lives.

It's up to us to take care of the planet. Sometimes humans hurt the environment with their actions, but there are many ways you can help out. This lesson has lots of ideas for ways to share our Earth. We can help both the people and environment around us. How many more ways to help can you think of?

Social Studies Vocabulary

habitat

tolerant

◀ It is important to protect our planet and its global community.

 Civics  Geography

1. Help Fight Air Pollution

You've seen how some people have tried to protect the environment. Let's look at some ways you can help.

One way to protect the environment is to fight air pollution. Cars are a major source of air pollution. So, you can help reduce air pollution by cutting down on how much you ride in cars.

Often, there are other ways of getting where you want to go. Instead of riding in a car, you might be able to take a bus, a train, or a subway. Maybe you could ride a bike or walk.

Do you still need a car to get where you are going? Try to find other people who are going to the same place. Then you can ride together in one car.

Biking, instead of using cars, helps fight air pollution.

2. Make Less Waste

A second way to help protect the environment is to make less waste. Most of our garbage goes into dumps called landfills. Many people worry that the waste in landfills can harm our air, soil, and water. Some places are running out of room to build new landfills.

How can you make less waste? Keep in mind the three R's: reduce, reuse, and recycle.

Reduce means to use less of things that will make waste. For example, your family can make less cardboard waste by buying one large box of cereal instead of several small ones. Your family can reduce toxic waste, too. When you buy products such as household cleaners, look for ones that don't have toxic chemicals in them.

Reuse means to use things more than once. Use both sides of a sheet of paper before you recycle it. Try making arts and crafts from materials instead of throwing them away.

Recycle means to save waste so it can be used again to make new products. In many places, you can recycle cans, bottles, newspapers, and other materials.

Is there a recycling program where you live?

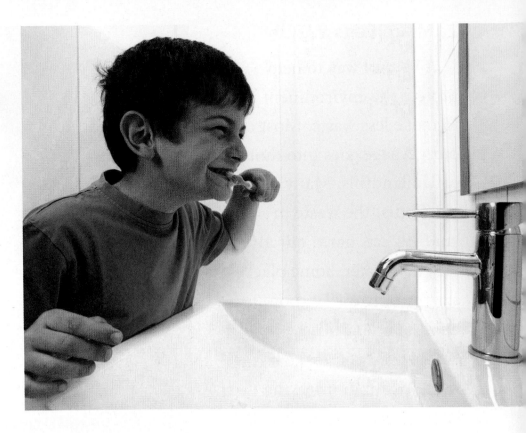

How many ways can you think of to save water?

3. Help Save Energy and Water

A third way to help protect the environment is to save precious resources. Two of these resources are energy and water.

Remember, nonrenewable sources of energy cannot be replaced in a short time. And even fresh water may become scarce.

You can help by using energy wisely. Turn off lights when you leave a room. Turn off televisions and computers when no one is using them. In cold weather, put on a sweater instead of turning up the heat.

Use water wisely, too. Take shorter showers, and don't leave the water running when you brush your teeth. If you have a hose, use a nozzle you can turn off when you lay the hose down. Tell your school or city about sprinklers that are broken or that are watering the sidewalk instead of grass and plants.

4. Help Keep Animals Safe

We share the planet with many kinds of wildlife. Birds and other animals need our help to survive. Here are three ways that people can help keep animals safe—even animals that live far away from you.

What can you do to protect these animals?

First, buy food that has been caught or raised safely. For example, some nets used to catch tuna also trap and kill dolphins. But other nets are designed to allow dolphins to escape. Your family can help save dolphins by knowing what brands of tuna keep dolphins safe.

Second, don't buy products made from endangered animals. Some examples are coats made from fur, decorations made with ivory from elephants, and belts made of crocodile skins. Not buying these can keep animals safe.

Third, find out about dangers to wildlife in your area. For example, some chemicals used on grass and other plants can poison birds. If you have a garden or yard, learn how to make it a safer place for wildlife.

5. Help Save Animal Habitats

habitat a place where particular animals live

You also can help animals by saving their **habitats**. Habitats are places where particular animals live, such as the forest or the seashore.

We often spoil animal habitats with our trash. Drinks are sometimes sold with plastic rings that hold bottles or cans together. Birds and other animals can get tangled in these rings. Animals can also choke on old balloons and other litter. Plastic bags that get washed into the ocean can harm fish and birds. So, don't be a litterbug! Even better, take along a trash bag when you go to a park or a beach, and pick up any litter you find.

You also can support groups that work to save animal habitats around the world. You can find many of these groups on the Internet. Some groups even have kids' clubs you can join.

Picking up litter is one way to help wildlife.

6. Share with Other People

People in friendly communities help one another. Nearly all of us can do something to help others in our global community.

One way to help is by sharing the things we have. If you have old clothes, don't throw them away. Maybe someone else in your family can use the clothes you've outgrown. Or you can give them to groups that collect clothes for people in need.

Other groups collect food or toys for families who can't afford to buy them. You may have seen collection barrels at your supermarket or school. Don't pass them by! You might have canned food in your kitchen that your family can give away. Or you might be able to save up to buy a toy or some food. Even one can of food can be a big help to someone.

Do you have food drives where you live?

UNICEF sends help to children around the world.

7. Lend a Helping Hand

Many groups bring people together to lend others a helping hand. You can help others by joining a group that's right for you.

One such group might be UNICEF (pronounced YOO-nih-sehf). UNICEF helps needy children around the world. Every Halloween, thousands of kids in the United States trick-or-treat to collect money for UNICEF instead of candy for themselves.

One town in California has a group of children who raise money to help youth in need around the world. They provide books, help fund treatment for the sick, and even have a scholarship for children interested in the arts. If you can't find a group to join, then maybe you can start one.

8. Treat Others with Respect

Everyone needs respect. You can make a big difference just by being **tolerant** of others. Being tolerant means respecting people even if they're different from you.

It's hurtful to make fun of others or to harm them because of how they look, dress, or talk. Act kindly instead. If you see people who are not being tolerant of others, then speak up. Remind them that everyone deserves respect.

Take time to learn about other people. The more you know about others, the more you will respect them. Talk to new people in your school or town. You might even try becoming pen pals with a child in another country.

tolerant respectful of other people even if they are different than you

No matter how someone looks or acts, you should treat them with respect.

9. Help Make Changes to Improve the World

How can you start helping the world? First, find a problem that interests you. It may be one from this lesson or something very different.

Asking questions about the problem is a great way to start. Ask questions like: what is causing the problem? And what is being done to stop it? If you were interested in protecting wildlife, you might ask: how are humans putting some animals in danger? Or why is it important to help these animals? Think of other questions you can ask.

There are many places to look for the answers to these questions. Web sites online are a great source for information. Be careful, though, because not everything you see online is true. Some Web sites might be written by someone who is not informed on the issues.

Books and magazines are helpful, too. Like Web sites, some are more reliable than others. You also can ask adults who may know more, like your parents or teacher.

The Internet is a good place to start finding information.

Keep an open mind when finding answers. People have many opinions, so different sources may give you different answers. Pay attention to who is providing the information. Look for evidence that supports the answer. Your job is to decide which answer is best.

Now, it is time to use what you know. You can gather other students who also want to protect animals. People are more likely to listen to a large group than a small group.

There are many ways to make change. You can try to spread the message to others about the problem. You could put up signs telling people how they can help the wildlife. You can try to raise money for the cause.

To make a change, you can inform other people about the problem.

You even can talk to people in the government. They could pass a law that helps animals. This is hard to do, but is one of the greatest changes you can make.

Lesson Summary

We are all members of the global community. There are things you can do to take care of the planet. You can help protect the environment, share things with other people, and get involved with organizations that help others.

There are many problems that you can help solve. You can choose a topic that interests you. You can ask questions about the topic and look for answers to the questions. You can try to make a difference in the world!

Learning About Others Through Art

Many countries share our Earth. But people sometimes dislike or fear those who live in other places. How can art help people around the world learn about one another?

People in different countries have different ways of life. They have their own governments and laws. They speak their own languages. It can be hard for them to know what people in other places are like.

Think of the United States and China, a country in Asia. Thousands of miles of ocean lie between these two countries. Most Chinese will never see the United States, and most Americans will never see China. So how can people in these places get to know one another? One way is through art.

This painting by Chen Lian Xing shows Chinese women decorating kites.

This painting by Chen Jiaqi shows a scene of family life in China.

Look at the painting that shows two women decorating kites in China. Notice the clothes they are wearing and the tools they are using. What does this scene tell you about Chinese culture? How is the scene alike or different from one that you might see in the United States?

The painting was made by a Chinese artist named Chen Lian Xing. His paintings show what life is like in the Chinese countryside.

The painting of family life also comes from China. What can you guess about the family members from details in the painting? What can you guess about the artist? What might he want you to feel about this family?

These paintings and many like them are available for people all over the world to look at, including people in the United States. When Americans see these pictures, they learn about people in China and about their lives. What are some things Americans might learn that they didn't know before?

A painting of Daniel Boone leading settlers through the mountains.

People in China are also learning about life in the United States. In 2007, there was an art show in China called *Art in America*, where more than 100 paintings were on display. They showed scenes in the United States from the year 1700 to today.

One painting showed George Washington. Another showed a famous pioneer named Daniel Boone. In the painting, Boone is leading settlers through a gap in some mountains.

Visitors also saw a painting of the Statue of Liberty and a painting of a clown with a drum. One picture showed a big sign saying "Hollywood." Hollywood is famous for being a place where American movies are made.

Many visitors were excited. People in China had never seen so much American art in one show. The show gave them an opportunity to learn about the United States.

Learning is what shows like these are all about. That is why the governments of China and the United States have agreed to share their art with each other. Art can teach us about other cultures and show us what is different and special about another country. Art can also show us how much we have in common with other people around the world.

In this way, art can help the world's people understand one another better. This may help us live together more peacefully as part of the global community. ◆

American art being shown in China.

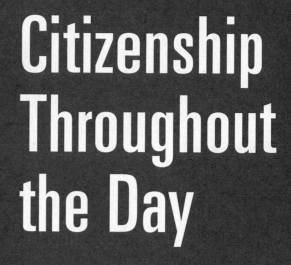

Citizenship Throughout the Day

You are a member of your family, school, and community. Each is a type of group. Being a citizen is like being part of a very large group. A citizen has certain rights. But there are also responsibilities for everyone everywhere. You can show good citizenship throughout the day at home, in your school, and in your community.

 Civics   Geography   History

The Pledge of Allegiance is a promise to respect the values that the flag stands for.

What Citizenship Means

A citizen is someone who has a right to live in a certain place. If you were born in the United States, then you are a U.S. citizen. If your parents are U.S. citizens, then you are, too. Does your family come from another country? If so, you may be a citizen of that country, this country, or both!

Citizens have many other rights as well. In fact, the United States was started by people who wanted to protect their rights. The Constitution lists many of these rights. But being a citizen doesn't just mean having rights. Citizens have responsibilities, too. For example, citizens must obey the law, and most must pay taxes. And all citizens must respect the values of our country. You promise to do this whenever you say the Pledge of Allegiance or sing the national anthem.

A big part of citizenship is doing our share to protect the things that all of us need and care about. We call things that are good for everyone in a community the common good. For instance, we all want our communities to be clean. If just one person litters, it spoils things for everyone. If people didn't pay taxes, then we wouldn't have money to pay for public services.

Look at this table. It shows some of the main rights and responsibilities of U.S. citizens. Together, these rights and responsibilities make up the idea of citizenship. A few, such as the right to vote, will apply to you when you are old enough. But most of them are part of your life right now. You can apply many of these rights and responsibilities to what you do at school, in the community, and at home. Let's take a closer look at how you can show good citizenship every day.

Some Rights and Responsibilities of U.S. Citizens	
Rights	**Responsibilities**
• To speak freely • To practice the religion of your choice • To gather peacefully with other people • To own property • To be safe from harm • To vote • To have a trial by jury	• To be loyal to your country and its values, especially freedom and equality • To care for the common good • To obey the law • To respect the rights and property of others • To pay taxes • To vote • To serve on juries

At School

During the school year, you spend a big part of your day at school. You have many chances to show good citizenship during this time.

To begin with, you can obey the rules. Schools have rules for the same reason that communities have laws. Rules help people get along. They protect both the common good and each person's rights. For instance, your school probably has rules about treating other people and their property with respect. And you have the right to be treated with respect, too.

Voting is a big part of citizenship.

Taking part in making decisions is a big part of citizenship. Do you elect leaders for your class, or for clubs or groups? Do you sometimes get to vote on projects or rules for your class or your school? Do you listen carefully to other people's points of view? If so, you're practicing good citizenship.

Helping other students is one way to be a good citizen at school.

You can also do things for the common good. Could some of your schoolmates use a helping hand? Are there problems at your school that you can help solve? Here are a few examples of things that students like you have done:

- Students at one school created illustrated books for kindergarteners. The books helped the young children learn about their new school.

- A group of third graders had a problem with bullies on the school bus. The third graders designed a program for bus safety. They worked together with older students, school officials, parents, and bus drivers.

- Many students tutor younger students in reading and other subjects.

Your school may have other projects or programs you can get involved in. Or you could start one yourself. Being a leader is another way to show good citizenship.

Members of a jury listen to a lawyer in court.

In the Community

You spend part of almost every day out in your community. Even if you're just shopping or going to a playground, you have both rights and responsibilities. For example, you have the right to speak and act freely as long as you respect the rights of others. You have a responsibility to obey the law. You have a responsibility to respect the property of others.

Some of your rights and responsibilities will change as you get older. When you have a job, you'll pay taxes on money you earn. As an adult, you will sometimes be expected to serve on a jury. A jury is a group of citizens who decide a case in court. You'll also have the right—and the responsibility—to vote. You may work to help elect a candidate. You may even run for office yourself.

Meanwhile, you can start right now to work for the common good in your town or city. You might work on a project such as helping to clean up a public park. Or you might start your own project. One group of third graders made a map of the safety features in their neighborhood. The map showed things like fire hydrants and telephones. Another group of students worked at a soup kitchen. They spent a day giving out food to hungry and homeless people.

You can also show citizenship by taking part in patriotic activities. Patriotism means love of your country. Many patriotic activities take place on holidays. Even going to see a Fourth of July parade in your community can be an act of citizenship. You can learn about other holidays that honor our country. What are some holidays you and your family celebrate?

Sometimes being a good citizen can be fun!

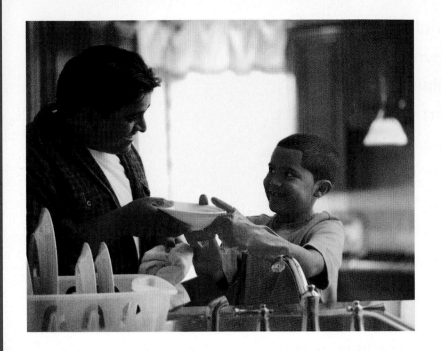

At home, good citizenship can mean helping out with chores.

At Home

You begin and end most days at home. Would you be surprised to find out that citizenship is part of your day there, too?

You probably have some rules at home. These rules help people live together, just as rules and laws do at school and in your community. So your first responsibility is to obey the rules.

A second responsibility is to show respect for others' rights and property. Help to take care of the space you share with others. It's the same idea as helping to keep the community clean so everyone can enjoy it.

A third responsibility is to tell the truth. Telling the truth means not telling lies. You keep your promises and admit when you are wrong. Have you ever played outside instead of doing your homework? What did you tell your parent? Telling the truth can sometimes be hard, especially if you've made a mistake.

Good citizens need to be able to cooperate. They must learn to listen to other points of view. They must learn to compromise for the common good. And they must learn to settle disagreements peacefully. You can practice all these parts of citizenship at home.

You can also help your family do its part in the community. For example, good citizens know what is happening in their community. They read or watch the news. They talk about the problems of the day. They speak up if they see a person being wronged. You may be able to help encourage this part of citizenship in your home.

That is just what one group of students did. They created a plan to encourage discussions during their families' dinnertimes. First, they brainstormed questions for the family to talk about during dinner. Then, they brought the questions home. Community organizations loved the idea, so they helped to support it.

As you can see, you can make citizenship a part of your life throughout the day. By now you probably have some ideas of your own. Why don't you write them down and start acting on them today?

For this family, dinnertime is a chance to talk about the news of the day.

Some Major Holidays in the United States

Holiday	Date	Purpose of Holiday
Martin Luther King Jr. Day	3rd Monday in January	To honor the birthday of civil rights leader Martin Luther King Jr.
Presidents' Day	3rd Monday in February	To honor all past U.S. presidents
Memorial Day	Last Monday in May	To remember Americans killed in wars
Independence Day	July 4	To celebrate the approval of the Declaration of Independence
Labor Day	1st Monday in September	To honor the country's working people
Columbus Day	1st Monday in October	To remember the day Christopher Columbus arrived in North America
Veterans Day	November 11	To honor Americans who have fought in wars
Thanksgiving Day	4th Thursday in November	To remember a feast of thanksgiving held by the Pilgrims (early settlers) and American Indians in 1621

The Pledge of Allegiance

I pledge allegiance to the Flag
of the United States of America,
and to the Republic
for which it stands,
one Nation under God, indivisible,
with liberty and justice for all.

The Star-Spangled Banner

Francis Scott Key wrote the words to "The Star-Spangled Banner" in 1814. The U.S. Congress made this song our national anthem in 1931. Here is the first verse.

Oh, say can you see, by the dawn's early light,
What so proudly we hailed at the twilight's last gleaming?
Whose broad stripes and bright stars, through the perilous fight,
O'er the ramparts we watched, were so gallantly streaming?
And the rockets' red glare, the bombs bursting in air,
Gave proof through the night that our flag was still there.
O say, does that star-spangled banner yet wave
O'er the land of the free and the home of the brave?

Solving Problems in School and Your Community

Asking Compelling Questions

Good citizens ask questions. They talk about their questions on television, in newspapers, and online. You can be a good citizen by asking questions, too!

Compelling questions are the questions you just need to know the answers to. They make you want to find answers. For example, one question might be "How can we make sure that everyone can learn to swim?"

Compelling questions do not have easy answers. So it helps to ask supporting questions to help answer them. Here are some supporting questions. "What fraction of third graders in my school knows how to swim?" "How is a private pool different from a public pool?" "Do communities with public pools charge citizens to use them?" "Are there other places nearby where children can swim?"

compelling question
a question you just need to know the answer to

Compelling questions are interesting questions. Thinking of supporting questions will help you answer them.

A librarian can help you find sources of information.

Finding Helpful Sources

You answer questions by using sources. Think about the swimming questions. A town or city Web site might be a helpful source. An expert, such as a lifeguard, could also be helpful. A library book about learning to swim might help.

A **primary source** of an event is an object created by someone who was there. Photos, notebooks, and letters can be primary sources. You might find a newspaper written on the day a public pool opened long ago. This could be a helpful primary source.

Knowing who wrote or made a source helps you decide if it is helpful. A person who is an expert on parks or pools is likely to have good information.

Facts and Opinions

Some sources only give facts. A **fact** is a true piece of information. A map of swimming lakes at state parks contains facts. Others may mix facts with opinions. An **opinion** is what someone thinks or believes. What's your opinion about whether everyone should learn to swim? When you use sources, understand whether they give facts, opinions, or both.

primary source an object created by someone who was at an event

fact a true piece of information

opinion what someone thinks or believes

You can communicate claims and evidence in many ways. One way is by giving a talk to your class.

evidence the facts you use to back up your claim

Making Claims and Using Evidence

By now you have collected some facts. You have answered your supporting questions. Now you are ready to come up with an answer to your compelling question, "How can we make sure that everyone can learn to swim?"

Your answer will be a claim supported with facts. Your claim might be, "Our community should have a place to give free swimming lessons." The facts you use to back up your claim are called **evidence**. One fact could be that people are safer if they know how to swim. Another could be that swimming is good exercise.

Communicating Conclusions

There are many ways to present your claims and evidence. You might give a talk to your class. You could also hold a debate. In a debate, there can be two teams of students. One team is for a claim, and the other team is against the claim.

You can also communicate with writing, drawings, and photos. They can be presented on a poster or a class Web page.

Taking Informed Action

Good citizens take action to help solve problems. Citizens can volunteer to help their community. They can write letters to the editor of a newspaper. They can write a petition. People who agree will sign the petition. The petition can be presented to community leaders.

Even students can make a difference. What if you wanted to finds ways to help more people learn to swim? You can use what you learned from helpful sources. You can share your ideas in school and outside school. What actions could you take alone? What actions could you take with others?

You can take action by sharing your conclusions about a problem. How would you take action to make sure everyone can learn to swim?

United States Physical Map

CANADA

CASCADE RANGE

Washington

Columbia River

45°N

Missouri River

Montana

North Dakota

Oregon

Idaho

ROCKY MOUNTAINS

Wyoming

South Dakota

GREAT PLAINS

40°N
125°W

SIERRA NEVADA

Nevada

Great Salt Lake

Utah

Colorado

Nebraska

Kansas

35°N

California

Colorado River

Arizona

New Mexico

PACIFIC OCEAN

120°W

Texas

Rio Grande

MEXICO

Alaska

70°
120°W

ARCTIC OCEAN

Bering Strait

Alaska

60°N
170°W

Gulf of Alaska

PACIFIC OCEAN

150°W   140°W

160°W

0   400 miles

0   400 kilometers

Hawaii

160°W

Kauai

Niihau

Oahu

Molokai

Lanai

Maui

Kahoolawe

PACIFIC OCEAN

20°N

Hawaii

0   150 miles

0   150 kilometers

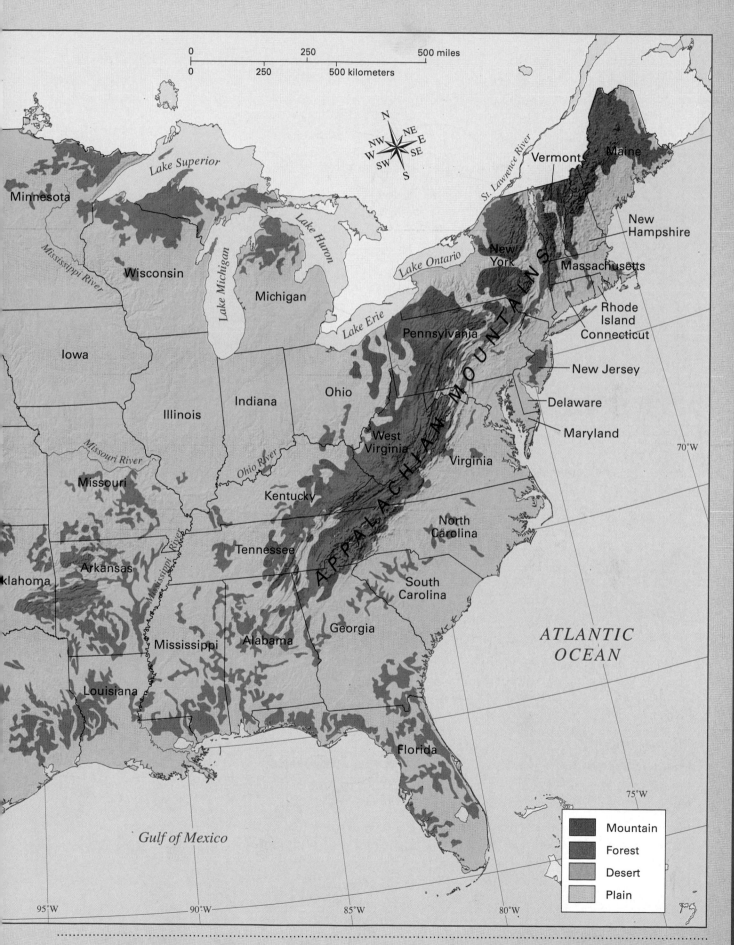

Minnesota

Lake Superior

Wisconsin

Lake Huron

Michigan

Lake Michigan

Lake Ontario

Mississippi River

Iowa

Lake Erie

Pennsylvania

New York

Vermont

Maine

St. Lawrence River

New Hampshire

Massachusetts

Rhode Island

Connecticut

New Jersey

Delaware

Maryland

Illinois

Indiana

Ohio

Missouri River

West Virginia

Ohio River

Virginia

70°W

Missouri

Kentucky

Mississippi River

North Carolina

Tennessee

Arkansas

klahoma

South Carolina

Mississippi

Alabama

Georgia

ATLANTIC OCEAN

Louisiana

Florida

Gulf of Mexico

75°W

N
NW NE
W E
SW SE
S

0   250   500 miles
0   250   500 kilometers

	Mountain
	Forest
	Desert
	Plain

95°W   90°W   85°W   80°W

United States Political Map

CANADA

Washington
★ Olympia

★ Salem

Oregon

Helena
★
Montana

North
Dakota
★
Bismarck

South
Dakota
Pierre ★

45°N

★ Boise
Idaho

Wyoming

125°W
40°N

Cheyenne
★

Nebraska

Sacramento
★

★ Carson City
Nevada

Salt Lake
★ City

Utah

Denver
★

Colorado

Kansas

California

35°N

Arizona
★ Phoenix

Santa Fe
★

New Mexico

Oklahoma
City
★

PACIFIC
OCEAN

120°W

Texas

Austin
★

ARCTIC OCEAN
70°N

Alaska

160°W
Kauai

Niihau

Oahu

Honolulu

Hawaii

PACIFIC
OCEAN

Molokai

Maui
Lanai
Kahoolawe

60°N
170°W

PACIFIC
OCEAN

Juneau
★

150°W   140°W

20°N

MEXICO

160°W

0   400 miles
0   400 kilometers

0   150 miles
0   150 kilometers

Hawaii

Scale:
0 — 250 — 500 miles
0 — 250 — 500 kilometers

N NE E SE S SW W NW (compass rose)

Minnesota

★ St. Paul

Wisconsin

★ Madison

Michigan

★ Lansing

Iowa

★ Des Moines

Lincoln

Illinois

★ Springfield

Indiana

★ Indianapolis

Ohio

★ Columbus

Pennsylvania

Harrisburg ★

New York

Albany ★

New Hampshire

Vermont

★ Montpelier

Maine

★ Augusta

★ Concord

Boston

Massachusetts

Hartford ★ ★ Providence

Rhode Island

Connecticut

★ Trenton

New Jersey

70°W

Annapolis ★ Dover

Delaware

✪ Washington D.C.

Maryland

West Virginia

★ Charleston

Virginia

Richmond ★

70°W

★ Topeka

Jefferson City ★

Missouri

Kentucky

★ Frankfort

★ Nashville

Tennessee

North Carolina

Raleigh ★

South Carolina

Columbia ★

klahoma

Arkansas

Little Rock ★

Mississippi

★ Jackson

Alabama

Montgomery ★

Georgia

Atlanta ★

ATLANTIC OCEAN

Louisiana

Baton Rouge ★

★ Tallahassee

Florida

Gulf of Mexico

95°W   90°W   85°W   80°W   75°W

| ✪ | U.S. capital |
| ★ | State capital |

World Physical Map

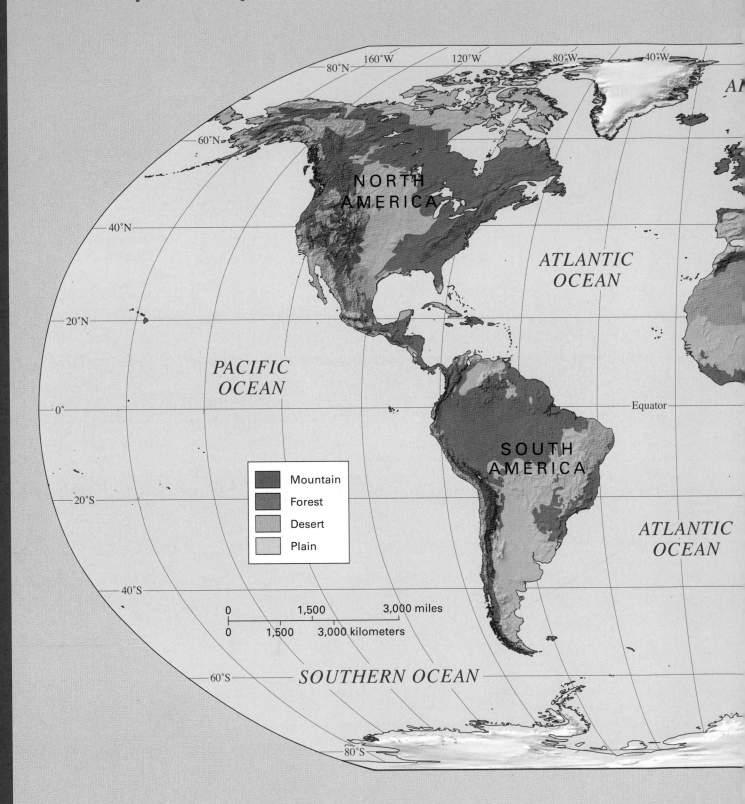

80°N
160°W   120°W   80°W   40°W

60°N

40°N

NORTH
AMERICA

ATLANTIC
OCEAN

20°N

PACIFIC
OCEAN

0°

Equator

SOUTH
AMERICA

	Mountain
	Forest
	Desert
	Plain

20°S

ATLANTIC
OCEAN

40°S

0		1,500		3,000 miles
0	1,500		3,000 kilometers	

60°S   SOUTHERN OCEAN

80°S

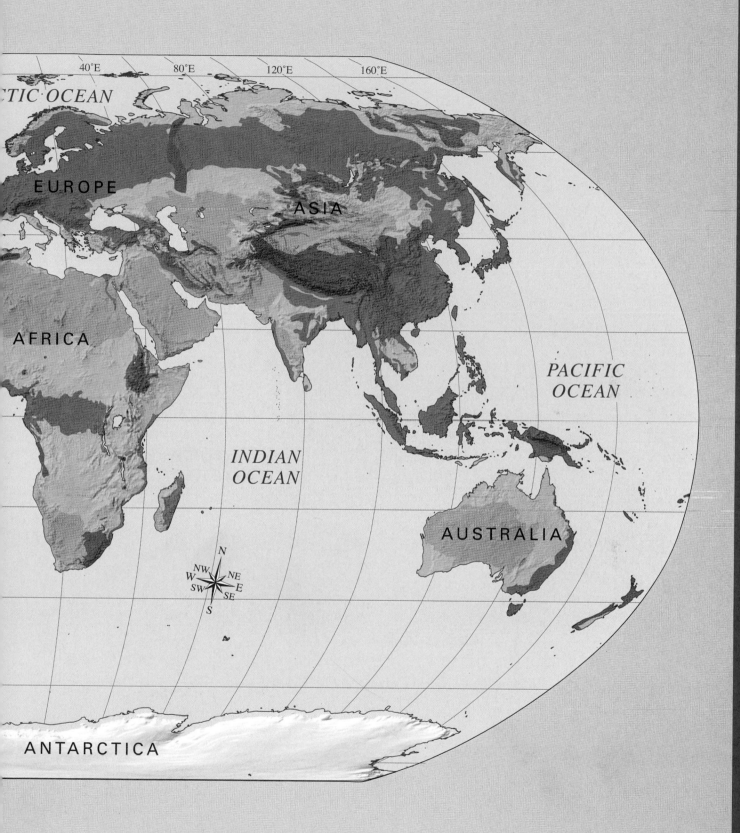

40°E 80°E 120°E 160°E

CTIC OCEAN

EUROPE

ASIA

AFRICA

PACIFIC
OCEAN

INDIAN
OCEAN

AUSTRALIA

N
NW   NE
W   E
SW   SE
S

ANTARCTICA

World Political Map

80°N   160°W   120°W   80°W   40°W

A.

60°N

NORTH
AMERICA

ATLANTIC
OCEAN

40°N

PACIFIC
OCEAN

20°N

0°

Equator

SOUTH
AMERICA

20°S

ATLANTIC
OCEAN

0   1,500   3,000 miles

40°S

0   1,500   3,000 kilometers

60°S   *SOUTHERN OCEAN*

80°S

CTIC OCEAN

EUROPE

AFRICA

ASIA

40°E 80°E 120°E 160°E

PACIFIC
OCEAN

INDIAN
OCEAN

AUSTRALIA

N
NW NE
W E
SW SE
S

ANTARCTICA

A

adapt   to change ways of living to fit an environment

B

ballot   a form on which people mark their votes in an election

Bill of Rights   a part of the Constitution that protects the rights and freedoms of Americans

border   the line where one place, such as a state or country, ends and another begins

boycott   when people refuse to buy products from a certain business

budget   a plan for how to use money

C

canal   a waterway made by humans

candidate   a person who tries to get elected to do a job in government for a community

canyon   a deep, narrow valley with steep sides

capital   the city where the government of a country or state meets

cardinal direction   one of the four main directions: north, east, south, and west

charity   a group that helps raise money for people who need it

citizen   a person who has the right to live in a certain place

citizenship   the rights and responsibilities of citizens

city hall   the building where the offices of a community's government are located

civil rights   rights a person has as a citizen

climate   the weather in a place, measured over time

climate change   a rise or fall in Earth's temperature over time

common good   the things that are good for everyone in a community

compelling question   a question you just need to know the answer to

conservation   the careful use of natural resources

Constitution   the document that sets up the basic rules of the United States government

continent   one of the seven large bodies of land on Earth

country   an area of land that has its own government

culture   a way of life shared by a group of people

D

Declaration of Independence   a document that said that the United States is free from the rule of Great Britain

demand   the total amount of a good or service that customers will buy at all prices

demonstration   a gathering of people to show shared feelings or opinions

disabled   not being able to do an everyday thing, such as walk, in the same way that most people can

discriminate   to treat people unfairly because they belong to a different group

diverse made up of different groups of people and cultures

donate give money or goods to someone in need

E

economy the system in which goods and services are bought and sold

entrepreneur someone who helps start and manage a new business

evidence the facts you use to back up your claim

environment Earth's air, water, soil, and living things

equator the imaginary line that divides Earth into the Northern and Southern hemispheres

F

fact a true piece of information

federal government the national government of the United States

first responder a person trained to give help at the scene of an emergency

fossil fuel a fuel that comes from the fossils, or remains, of plants or animals

free market economy an economy where choices are left up to each buyer and seller

G

geography the study of Earth—its spaces, land, water, air, and people

global trade the buying and selling of goods and services between countries around the world

goods items that can be bought, sold, and traded, such as food and computers

government a group that helps run a community, state, or country

H

habitat a place where particular animals live

I

immigrant a person who comes from another place to live in a country

incentive something that leads a person to make a certain choice

interest extra money that you make from saving money at a bank

invest using money in the hopes of making more money in the future

L

legislature the part of the government that makes laws

local government the government of a city, town, county, or other area in the United States that is smaller than a state

M

map key a feature that explains what the symbols on a map stand for

manufactured made with machines

market a place where buyers and sellers come together

migrant worker someone who moves from place to place to get work

militia an army made up of soldiers who serve during emergencies

N

natural disaster an event in nature, such as an earthquake or flood, that causes great harm

natural hazard a force of nature that shapes Earth

natural resource a useful item that comes from nature, such as wood from trees

nonrenewable resource a natural resource that cannot be made again in a short time

O

ocean one of the five largest bodies of water on Earth

opinion what someone thinks or believes

P

peaceful done without hurting others or their property

physical feature a natural feature of Earth's surface, such as a mountain, plain, lake, or river

physical geography the physical features, climate, and natural resources of a place

primary source an object created by someone who was at an event

prime meridian the imaginary line that divides Earth into the Eastern and Western hemispheres

private service a service that is provided for money by a business

profit the amount of money earned by a business after costs are removed

pollution anything that makes air, water, or soil dirty or unsafe

public service a service, such as a public library, that is offered by a community to everyone

public works things such as roads, water pipes, and streetlights that everyone in a community uses

R

region an area with certain common features that set it apart from other areas

register to sign up to vote

renewable resource a natural resource, such as sunlight, that does not get used up

republic a type of government in which the citizens elect their leaders to represent them

S

scale a feature used to figure out distances on a map

scarcity when people want more things than they can actually have

services tasks you pay someone to do for you

special-purpose map a map that shows information about a single topic

state one of the 50 main areas with their own governments that make up the United States

state government the government of one of the states of the United States

strike   when workers stop working to try to get something they want, such as better pay

suburb   a community that grows up on the edge of a city

supply   the total amount of a good or service available to buy

symbol   an object that stands for something else (for example, the Liberty Bell is a symbol of freedom)

T

tax   money that people pay to a government

tolerant   respectful of other people even if they are different than you

toxic waste   poisonous trash or garbage

tradition   something that people do together year after year

V

volunteer   a person who agrees to do a task without being paid for it

Cover and Title Page
Shutterstock

Front Matter
vi L: Thinkstock **vi R:** Thinkstock
vii: Thinkstock **viii:** Thinkstock
viii: Thinkstock **ix:** Thinkstock
ix: Thinkstock **xii:** NASA
xii: Thinkstock **xii:** Bambi L.
Dingman/Dreamstime **xiii:** Library
of Congress **xiii:** blickwinkel/
Alamy **xiii:** Thinkstock **xiv:**
Bruno Morandi/Corbis **xiv:**
iStockphoto **xiv:** Thinkstock
xv: iStockphoto **xv:** Thinkstock
xv: Shutterstock **xvi:** Steven
Greaves/Corbis **xvi:** Shutterstock
xvi: Sergey Mostovoy/Dreamstime
xvi: Thinkstock **xvii:** Shutterstock
1: The Granger Collection, NYC

Lesson 1
2: NASA **4:** Corbis **7:** Getty
Images **8:** Shutterstock **10:** NASA
12–13: Thinkstock **12 L:** Ilene
MacDonald/Alamy **13 R:** Ilene
MacDonald/Alamy **14:** Wikimedia
15 T: Library of Congress
16 T: Shutterstock **17 T:** The Granger
Collection, NYC **17 B:** Shutterstock

Lesson 2
18: Thinkstock **20:** Thinkstock
21 L: Thinkstock **21 R:** Shutterstock
22: Robert Marmion/Alamy
24: Shutterstock **25:** Getty Images
26: Thinkstock **27:** Getty Images
28: Thinkstock **29:** Vvp/Dreamstime
30: Library of Congress **31:** Blend
Images/Alamy **32:** Shutterstock
33: Thinkstock **34 T:** iStockphoto
34 B: iStockphoto **35:** iStockphoto

Lesson 3
36: Bambi L. Dingman/
Dreamstime **39:** Thinkstock
40: Jmaentz/Dreamstime
41: Leigh Prather/Dreamstime
42: Kitty Miller **43:** Thinkstock
44: iStockphoto **45:** Neutronman/
Dreamstime **46:** Getty Images
47: Matt Campbell-epa/Corbis
48: Thinkstock **49:** Wikimedia
50: iStockphoto **52:** Provided by
the SeaWiFS Project, NASA/
Goddard Space Flight Center,
and ORBIMAGE **55 R:** Welshi23/
Dreamstime

Lesson 4
56: Library of Congress **58:** Library
of Congress **59:** Library of
Congress **60:** Library of Congress
61: Library of Congress **62:** Library
of Congress **63:** Shutterstock
64: iStockphoto **65 L:** Library
of Congress **65 R:** Shutterstock
66: iStockphoto **67:** Ivy Close
Images/Alamy **68:** Getty Images
69: Nancy Nehring/Getty Images
72: Thinkstock **73:** Getty Images
74: Thinkstock **75:** iStockphoto

Lesson 5
76: blickwinkel/Alamy **78:** Library
of Congress **79:** MBI/Alamy
80 B: dbimages/Alamy **80 T:** Ufuk
Uyanik/Dreamstime **81:** Pierre
Arsenault/Alamy **82:** iStockphoto
83: Richard Levine/age fotostock/
Superstock **84:** Richard Gunion/
Dreamstime **85:** Purestock/
Alamy **86:** Sergio Vila/
Dreamstime **87:** Radius Images/
Alamy **88:** Crissy Pascual/
ZUMA Press/Corbis **89:** Sbukley/
Dreamstime **90:** Associated Press
91 B: iStockphoto **92 B:** Library of
Congress **93:** Library of Congress
94 B: Oldtime/Alamy **95:** The
Granger Collection, NYC

Lesson 6
96: Thinkstock **98:** iStockphoto
99: KidStock/Blend Images
100: Library of Congress
101: Shutterstock **102:** Shutterstock
103: Bettmann/Corbis
104: Bettmann/Corbis
105: iStockphoto **106:** Bettmann/
Corbis **107:** Galen Rowell/Corbis
108: PR Newswire/AP Images
109: Thinkstock **110 R:** Marty
Bahamonde/FEMA **111 T:** Win
Henderson/FEMA **111 B:** Jeff
Schmaltz, MODIS Rapid Response
Team, Nasa/GSFC **112:** Getty
Images **113:** Associated Press
115 B: Shutterstock

Lesson 7

116: Bruno Morandi/Corbis
118: Shutterstock **119:** Danita Delimont/Alamy **120 T:** Staffan Widstrand/Corbis **121:** Lawrence Migdale/Getty Images
122 B: Courtesy of Charles Shafsky **123:** Courtesy of Charles Shafsky **124 T:** Tadashi Miwa/ Getty Images **125:** Shutterstock
126 B: Getty Images
127: Shutterstock **128 T:** Damian Tully/Alamy **129:** Bill Bachman/ Alamy **130 B:** powderkeg stock/ Alamy **131:** Olusegun Otakoya/ Demotix/Corbis **132:** age fotostock/ Alamy **133 T:** age fotostock/Alamy
134: Gianni Dagli Orti/The Art Archive at Art Resource, NY
135: Konstantin Kalishko/Alamy
136: iStockphoto **137 T:** iStockphoto
137 B: Polka Dot Images/ Superstock

Lesson 8

138: iStockphoto **140:** Thinkstock
141: Thinkstock **142:** iStockphoto
143: iStockphoto **144:** Thinkstock
145: iStockphoto **146:** iStockphoto
147: Thinkstock **148:** Thinkstock
149: Kurhan/Dreamstime
150: Shutterstock **151 T:** Library of Congress **152:** Bettmann/ Corbis **153 T:** Library of Congress
153 B: Library of Congress
154: Pierre-yves Babelon/ Dreamstime **155:** Thinkstock

Lesson 9

156: Thinkstock **158:** iStockphoto
159: Thinkstock **160:** Arne9001/ Dreamstime **161 T:** Thinkstock
161 B: Thinkstock **162:** Thinkstock
164: Thinkstock **166 T:** Thinkstock
166 B: Thinkstock **167:** Shutterstock
168: Reuters/Corbis
169: iStockphoto **170:** Deborah Feingold/Corbis **171:** iStockphoto

Lesson 10

172: iStockphoto **174:** Thinkstock
175: Deyan Georgiev Authentic collection/Alamy
176: Thinkstock **177:** Thinkstock
178: Comaniciu Dan Dumitru/ Dreamstime **179:** Thinkstock
180: iStockphoto **181:** Thinkstock
182: Thinkstock **183 TL:** Thinkstock
183 TR: Thinkstock **183 BR:** Nitr/ Dreamstime **183 BL:** Steven Cukrov/Dreamstime **184:** Pavel Losevsky/Dreamstime **185 T:** Thinkstock

Lesson 11

186: Thinkstock
188 L: Thinkstock **188 R:** Thinkstock
189: Thinkstock **190:** Getty Images
191: Thinkstock **192:** Thinkstock
193: Pa2011/Dreamstime
194: iStockphoto **195:** iStockphoto
196: Thinkstock **197:** Thinkstock
199: Getty Images **200 L:** iStockphoto
200 R: iStockphoto **201:** Midhun Menon/Dreamstime

Lesson 12

202: Shutterstock **204:** Rmarmion/ Dreamstime **205:** Robert Kneschke/ Dreamstime **206:** iStockphoto
207: iStockphoto **208:** Thinkstock
209 L: Rafael Ben-Ari/ Alamy **209 R:** iStockphoto
210: Irina Brinza/Dreamstime
211: Steven Frame/Dreamstime
212: iStockphoto **213:** Monkey Business Images/Dreamstime
214: Photodisc/Getty Images
215: Wikimedia **216:** Ian Klein/ Dreamstime **217:** Image Source/ Alamy **218:** iStockphoto
219: iStockphoto **220:** Library of Congress **221 T:** The Granger Collection, NYC **221 B:** iStockphoto
222: iStockphoto **223:** Library of Congress

Lesson 13

224: Steven Greaves/Corbis
226: iStockphoto **227:** Getty Images
228: Getty Images **229:** Shutterstock
230: Tokyo Space Club/Corbis
231: Rmarmion/Dreamstime
232: Thinkstock **233:** John Roman/ Dreamstime **234:** Cultura Creative (RF)/Alamy **235:** Ilene MacDonald/ Alamy **236:** iStockphoto
237: Robhainer/Dreamstime
238 T: iStockphoto **238 C:** Thinkstock
238 B: Shutterstock **239:** iStockphoto
240: Library of Congress
241: National Archives **242 L:** Corbis
242 R: Leonard A. Williams/ National Geographic Society/ Corbis **243:** Glenn Nagel/ Dreamstime **244:** Bettmann/ Corbis **245 B:** Bettmann/Corbis
245 T: Library of Congress